How to use less water in your garden

A practical guide to waterwise Mediterranean style gardening worldwide

Dick Handscombe

ABOUT THE BOOK AND AUTHOR

This book is a practical book of interest to anyone gardening or having an allotment in a Mediterranean climate area or other parts of the world, including the UK, that have long periods of drought from time to time or where water is just getting more, or likely to get more and more expensive, or in short supply.

The book focuses on how to use less water and save and use rainwater better, to create attractive and productive home gardens of all sizes and allotments away from the home property. It will also be of interest to those responsible for municipal gardens.

It is written by Dick Handscombe who being now seventy seven years of age has seventy two years of gardening under his belt including twenty seven years in Spain. His first garden was on a dry heap of earth created in the front garden of his parent's house in west London when an unexploded bomb was dug up in 1942.He later gardened in a wide range of soils and regional rainfalls in Middlesex, Hertfordshire, Cheshire, Lancashire, Norfolk, Surrey, Berkshire and Holland before moving to Spain. While working in some thirty countries, and holidaying in ten more, he observed the various gardening practices particularly in relation to the conservation and use of water. He now tends a garden, allotment, olive grove and an untamed mountainside of wild plants in Spain.

During his residency in Spain there have been major changes in the pattern of rainfall, availability and price of both town and agricultural water which have required changes in gardening plantings and practices. These experiences led him to prepare this book *'How to use less water in your garden – A practical guide to waterwise Mediterranean style gardening wordwide'*.

..

Dedications

To my wives Ria and Clodagh who in succession joined and supported me during the past forty years in experimenting with ways of gardening as dry as possible in Spain and in travelling the world picking up novel ideas. Also to my and younger brother Bernard who with his gardening and agricultural oriented family have coped with Australia's dry Mediterranean style climates for forty years and my daughter Sophie who enjoyed a year of dry gardening on a kibbutz in Israel and since, with grandson George has who had to cope with long hose pipe bans in their colourful garden and on their productive allotment in the south of England.

Acknowledgements

The book is a brain dumping of all the related ideas included in my earlier gardening books and articles, plus those forgotten at the time but now recalled together with others dreamt up while compiling this book. Inevitably not all are unique to me and have been come across when visiting family and friends, when giving talks or coaching persons starting new gardens or modifying existing ones and when travelling the world on business or for pleasure. Having now had a personal garden for seventy two years and having recently had a seventy seventh birthday, some ideas go back a long way. It would be impossible to remember and list all the persons who have had an influence on the ideas included in this book but I thank them all for the lifelong stimulation of sharing gardening problems and identifying and trying out new solutions. But four family members must be highlighted, Clodagh my wife and gardening companion for some years, my younger brother Bernard living in Adelaide Australia who has swapped notes re South Australian and Spanish Mediterranean style gardening and agriculture, plus my long deceased father and grandfather with whom I first experienced gardening on dried out West London clay and cracked Hertfordshire chalk downs. Lastly my thanks go to neighbour Patricia Philson for reviewing the final draft and suggesting some important extra content.

Contents   Page

AUTHORS INTRODUCTION

' How to use less water in your garden' is a holistic and practical guide for use by individuals or groups interested in using less water on their gardens but still making them more beautiful restful healthy and productive places to live and work in, during both working and retirement years.

The book is a compilation of things I have done, seen done or would like to see done in gardens and allotments worldwide. Many of the ideas have been applied and tested in my garden allotment olive grove or those of family members, friends and clients. Others have been observed while working in some thirty countries worldwide and visiting a dozen more when undertaking study tours or holidays. The concepts and ideas explained are relevant to all sizes and forms of gardens whether around a villa, townhouse, on an apartment terrace or utilizing an allotment.

The issue is not new. From Neolithic times water has been harvested and used for growing things. In those days the numbers of individuals and families were few and often far apart, with the location of their cave or basic dwelling being determined by the location of springs and rivers. Over the millenniums shortages of water arose during and following periods of drought and as populations grew. At times people have starved, important annual crops have been lost and beautiful gardens severely damaged. Unfortunately the demand for water has not been matched by an effective harvesting of rain water in most parts of the world. Not only do major collection storage and distribution projects, plus projects for the purification and recycling of waste waters, fall short of projected demand. But most importantly the millions of new residential properties, built over the past thirty years in Spain and other Mediterranean situations, have not been required to continue the historic practice of collecting and storing water in storage tanks under or adjacent to the houses.

In addition many houses have been built on shallow rocky soil or tired agricultural land where the water retentive properties of the original rich fertile soil, improved annually with natural animal and bird fertilizer, was lost with the advent of chemical agriculture and gardening. In domestic gardens the problem has been exasperated by the planting of thirsty and hungry imported plants, which were largely not available twenty five years ago, when the plants in garden centres were mostly indigenous, naturalized, fairly drought resistant and sold in pots filled with growing mediums that enabled plants to be speedily established in garden soils.

As a result there are few places in the world that have not or will not, from time to time, experience water shortages affecting one's ability to develop and maintain a great lifestyle leisure garden and grow the family's food. I have lived in a coastal mountain village in Spain for the past twenty seven years. There are caves at either end which were occupied by early man from 25,000 and 27,000 BC respectively. The land we garden on for flowers herbs vegetables fruit and olives was monastery land from 1298 until 1836. Watering systems range from flooding from natural springs to drip tubing, from watering cans to hose pipes and just letting plants wait for the rain. During our residence climate variations have ranged from plus 47 degrees centigrade one summer seventeen years ago down to minus fifteen in March 2005, no rain fall for the past six months, a heaviest rainfall of 650 mm in 24 hours in November 1996 of which 240 fell in an hour and luckily we have only experienced only one disastrous hail storm. That bashed our collection of heritage squashes and tomatoes to smithereens. However in general we have very pleasant weather throughout the year and seasonally colourful and productive gardens and allotments can be created by respecting seasonal climate variations, especially the availability and use of rain falls.

Water is essential to life and potentially copiously available. But now many believe that the current worldwide phenomenon of global warming will increase the scale and frequency of local shortages, and thereby increase the number of gardens and allotments with an urgency for action. Whether permanent global warming is real or not, it is my personal experience during 77 years of living on this planet, 72 of them with gardening as a hobby and major retirement pastime and of visiting some forty countries worldwide, that the changes have been enormous already and time is not on our side.

I hope that this practical addition to the literature related to using less water in gardens and allotments, and of better retaining and using rain water, will help you create and maintain a better garden with significantly less expenditure on water, and persuade others to do likewise. More plants and produce with significantly less water is a real possibility and many of the ideas in the book have been used in my garden, allotment, olive grove and area of wild hillside in Spain.

The book is intended to be of benefit to amateur and professional gardeners and horticultural /landscaping students.

Dick Handscombe

Spain 2014

1. THE WATERWISE GARDENING CHALLENGE

Wherever one lives or works in the world scenic and edible plants need some water at each stage of their life cycle whether annuals biennials or perennials. But the trend is for too much water to be used while water becomes less available and more expensive, due to an exponential increase in demand. This increase caused by the increase in the number of persons living in houses with gardens, population growth and changes in the extent and seasonality of rainfall.

Yet rain water, the lifeline of life, and the growing of all types of plants in the world's gardens and allotments is free when it falls. But unfortunately most rainfall is not harvested, stored or distributed productively around gardens, retained by soils or used by plants when germinating growing and maturing. The problem is compounded by gardeners new to Mediterranean climate conditions attempting to establish temperate style gardens or subtropical type gardens with, in both cases, plants that require more water than native or long established imported and naturalised plants while drought conditions in gardens and allotments are becoming more frequent.

The 21st century challenge for gardeners is to be more water-wise by firstly being more thoughtful about the plants they plant, secondly taking more diligent steps to coach plants to establish deep root systems down into cool depths of moist soil, thirdly collecting storing and distributing rain water effectively and fourthly using purchased town or agricultural water more effectively. Each of these issues is examined in depth within this book.

Before reading further consider where your garden and gardening practices sit in the matrix that follows and in which direction your efforts have been moving.

		Low	Medium	High
Extent of planting of highly and moderately drought resistant indigenous and naturalized plants	High			Ultimate success
	Moderate			
	Low	Significant problems from day one		

Continuous diligent attempts to enable and coach plant roots to grow deeply downwards into deep damp soil rather than side-ways into wet surface soil.

Fig.1 Extent of success in establishing a scenically beautiful and productive garden that requires little watering and maintenance.

During the past twenty five years of gardening in Spain I have observed that:

- We now rarely experience summer thunder storms. They used to be monthly from May to August. As I write in the middle of May we had no measureable rainfall since last autumn, until a couple of weeks ago. Then we had just ten millimeters of dirty rain full of Saharan desert dust that left a thick coating on cars, terraces and plants. The fourteen day forecast suggests that there will be no more rain until the last two days of the month. Elderly villagers tell me that in their youth May was a very wet month with frequent storms.

- The autumn Gota Fria rains, like monsoon rains but on a smaller scale, used to fall without fail in mid September. But for the past ten years the first autumn rains have been getting later and later. In some years they have not fallen until well into November.

- Rainfall can be very localized. When we recently had just 5 millimetres twenty kilometres away rainfalls of up to 200 millimetres destroyed part of the rice crops.

- Some winters can now be called dry rather than wet although we are definitely living and gardening in a Mediterranean climate zone.

- If spring rains were sparse they used to make up for it over the first weekend in May. For some years we ran a long weekend walking camp which was twice washed out. This has not happened for the past few years. Springs that are said not to have stopped running since Roman and Arab times are definitely now running slower by mid-summer.

- Dependence on spring water for domestic water in our valley was changed to a borehole pump and reservoir in the 1950's. Increases in building activity and the number of summer residents in the late eighties and early nineties led to the need for residents to pay for a larger pump and reservoir tank. But in the pre-crisis building boom shortages of domestic water were again experienced as new building took precedence over residents needs.

- The sea is a degree or two warmer as in the last fifteen years there has been less rain water reaching the sea as run off from the land, through drains or from river estuaries.

- Inland, and in some coastal places, winter frosts have been harsher, even if only occasionally, following the record fortnight of well below zero frosts in March 2004 and 2005. In the past decade many fields of oranges have been abandoned due to frost damage and the shortage and cost of agricultural water.

- Many garden centres that had an adjacent nursery lost a high percentage, up to 90%, of their stock of plants during the 2005 frosts and as a result had to import more plants. Many of these were larger than normal and much more difficult to establish in average gardens. This trend has often continued.

- Droughts were severe in 2004/2005, 2007, 2008, 2012 and 2013. In places the impact on gardeners was more severe than the then amazing UK droughts of 1976 and 2011/12.

- Local agriculture has been progressively abandoned due to increases in the cost of agricultural water and chemicals, and the drying up of nearby springs.

- Water is being saved by importing animal and human foods from countries with more and less expensive water so we depend on rainfalls in developing countries to support our richer lifestyles. Maybe water will become a traded commodity.

- If another building boom starts in the next few years many expatriates and Spaniards will face water shortages again.

- Many towns and villages that established colorful flowering gardens alongside roads, in the centre islands of dual carriage way roads and on roundabouts a few years ago as tourist attraction, are now introducing designs and plantings that require less water.

Contact with gardening friends living in other countries around the Mediterranean Sea and further afield indicate similar experiences. The fundamental aim must therefore be to achieve more with less water both in rainy and dry seasons, wherever one is in the world. More in terms of germination growth and survival of plants including flowering and evergreen plants and trees, edible and aromatic herbs, fruit plants bushes and trees and vegetables of all types.

This will be achieved by a combination of decisions and actions related to the design, development, operation and maintenance of your villa or apartment garden, and perhaps a maturing allotment, as well as to public parks and intensive agriculture. As indicated in the contents list there are many wide ranging facets to the challenge. We have grouped them under a number of headings for ease of reading and recall, as the overall picture is like a complex jigsaw of interdependent issues.

As a start point 'Better and less expensive gardens' will be achieved by improving the soil, improved plant selection, more mulching, increasing the amount of rain water saved and it's better distribution, using less water, less work and by losing fewer plants etc..

Without taking corrective actions a relatively small percentage of the rain that falls and water used for watering will be actually taken in by the roots to support healthy cellular growth and extract nutrients from the soil.

From my personal experience the fourteen most important ways in which water is lost are:

1. Rain water is wasted. Most is not effectively harvested and used.

2. Water runs away across the surface of bone dry soil away from the plants being watered.

3. Water is lost by surface evaporation and by capillary action from lower levels in the soil as it dries out, especially on hot and windy days.

4. In dry weather water used to water plants is lost by suction into dry surrounding areas of soil.

5. If water absorbing and holding soils and composts are not developed a considerable amount of water can soak down through the soil and composts and drain away below the deepest roots.

6. Where thirsty and drought resistant plants are co-planted the latter get too much water and may attract bugs or even rot.

7. Attempting to establish very thirsty plants that do not survive hot sunny windy weather, even with copious watering in an otherwise sensible dry garden.

8. Attempting to establish large plants which need to establish deep roots in shallow soil over solid rock, rather than building raised beds.

9. Attempting to create English or tropical gardens in a Mediterranean climate situation.

10. Not shading containers of plants on hot apartment terraces and balconies and town house roof top terraces.

11. Water from springs or fountains and mains water is too often regarded as free or inexpensive and therefore is not used productively.

12. Without effective mulching around plants shrubs and trees water evaporates fast from dried out sunburnt soils.

13. Much rain water runs to uncultivated areas of the garden.

14. Hired gardeners play safe and use excess water, especially if working for absentee owners who arrive with little or no warning.

15. Rain and excessively used town water is allowed to run away onto other properties without maximising its potential use or storage within the perimeters of one's own land.

16. With water bottling companies buying up water mining rights it is becoming more difficult, in some country areas, to achieve permissions for the sinking and use of wells for domestic and garden water supplies.

Naturally the scale of the challenge and urgency for actions varies from situation to situation, and person to person. However all of us in the world can do something. Cumulatively that could add up to a much better world to live in, healthier gardens, better foods for many and a significant reduction in personal regional and national water costs. Waterwise or waterless gardening practices therefore make sense in all gardens, not just those Xeriscaped from day one. That is to landscape design a garden to minimize water requirements for their establishment and maintenance.

Water saving can be tackled on an individual or group basis. If you need the support of others to initiate actions set up a family, street, building, gardening club, allotment association group or circle as discussed later in Section 7.1. Recently it occurred to me that there is scope for 'Master Water Saving' awards in a similar way to the 'Master Composter' awards made in the UK by the Think Organic, ex HDRA, organisation.

Rather than just glancing through the book picking up ideas piecemeal see it as a general briefing or update on what is possible and also a workbook for selecting and prioritising personal aims and actions. Reading the book will help you recognise where water is already used wisely, season by season, and where it is regularly lost or poorly used with a real potential for meaningful savings.

Throughout the book when reference is made to a garden it means the area of land around a house or the area of apartment terraces and balconies. An allotment is regarded as an area of rented or borrowed land away from the house or apartment garden.

2. HARVESTING AND PRIORITISING IMPROVEMENT IDEAS

This book is intended to be a living book, one designed to stimulate changes in today's and tomorrow's gardening practices. It is a lifetime crop of ideas waiting for you to harvest those most relevant to your situation.

It is suggested that you read through the book from beginning to end ticking or circling those ideas that have some relevance to your own situation and numbering them for later reference and recall.

Then when you have read and marked up the book go back to the beginning and evaluate each of the ideas that had an appeal to you.

For objectivity it is suggested that you evaluate ideas on the basis of the following three criteria.

1. Potential for reducing the use of water – High, medium or low.

2. Ease of implementing the idea – High, medium or low.

3. Cost of implementation – Low, medium or high.

For me the first things to act on would be those that score High, High , Low

For such tasks I like to draw up a chart to help organize and evaluate the information. In this case may I suggest the following format.

With such a list and analysis you will have the possibility of developing a meaningful plan of action. A plan focused on making speedy and continuous savings in water and the time you spend on watering. The benefits will be achieved through improvements in your day to day gardening practices to achieve still achieve a delightful colourful scented and productive garden and/or allotment.

Collation and analysis of best ideas from the book for our garden						
No.	Ref.No. in book	Brief description of idea	Potent-ial savings H,M, L	Ease of doing H, M, L	Cost of doing H,M ,L	Priority for action H, M, L
1.	4.7.3	Place stone slabs over the roots of each of our climbing plants.	M	H	L	H
2.						
3.						
4.						
5.						
6.						

.

3. THE BENEFITS OF TAKING ACTION NOW

Reading through the book you will become more conscious of how important water is in both improving your garden and in preventing unnecessary problems. For instance when you make plant choices recognise which plants are naturally drought resistant and which are thirsty, and then prepare soils and plant accordingly. A list of the most drought resistant plants that we have experienced in Spain is provided in Appendices 4 and 5.

Also consciously modify your garden objectives layout and quality of soils to retain as much rain fall as possible when it falls before planting anything, or anything new in an existing garden. Then as the garden and/or allotment starts to be planted up get used to walking your land to check for water wastes and plants under stress. Start to think about preventing the substantial losses of uncollected and un-stored rain water and how the use of costly public water supplies could be reduced. Part 5 of the book discusses such issues. But these are not the only benefits.

Meaningful benefits and potential savings from reading and acting on the many ideas collated in the following sections of the book include:

- Less frustration with your garden.

- Less plants lost and less cost of replacements.

- Less time spent watering.

- Garden easier to leave when travelling away for extended periods.

- Lower water bills. Less money spent on purified towns water or tanker loads of agricultural water.

- Healthier plants with less problems and costs associated with deterring and killing off unwanted insects and fungi.

- Less erosion of soil and landscapes.

- A microclimate that allows one to experiment with new plants.

- Better edible flower, fruit, herb and vegetable harvests.

- A better all year round garden that matches the microclimate.

- A more perfumed garden as many drought resistant plants are perfumed.

- A possible reduction in the hours of work given to employed gardeners.

In respect to water savings measurements of before and after uses can be made by comparing meter readings, the time to fill a bucket, your invoiced water bills and reductions in the time you need to spend watering, especially during the hot summer months.

4. 250 PLUS WAYS OF REDUCING THE NEED TO USE WATER

As already emphasized, whatever local micro climate one lives in and whatever the size and complexity of one's garden allotment or apartment terraces there is scope to make significant reductions in the volume of water required to keep your future plants alive and thriving, especially during periods of drought. From day one think about Xeriscaping, the art and practice of gardening and growing with the minimum of water and ensure that you maximise the collection and use of rain water and the use of natural water from local springs and wells. Aim for a permanent reduction or at best the achievement of not needing to pay for piped chlorinated town water.

Here are two hundred possible practical actions to consider collated by twelve practical groupings. Naturally different ideas will appeal to different persons depending on whether their style of garden is a botanical garden with the largest collection of plants possible, a garden designed to live out in with mainly drought resistant plants once they mature, or a minimal garden with limited plantings.

4.1 The design and development of your garden.

There is no one way of preparing a garden in Mediterranean or other dry situations for gardens of many types are seen as great in the eyes of the beholder. Each of us may well have very different ideas to friends, neighbours and fellow members of gardening clubs and societies about how best to utilize a given site and microclimate. I therefore share below some personal concepts beliefs and practices, based on my personal experiences, for you to consider.

1. Increase your first thoughts about the percentage of the garden that will be covered by terraces, paths and stone/rock chippings. Consider the following guidelines.

Type of garden	% soil covered with terraces, pools and stone chippings	% soil covered with paths	% soil used for flowerbeds
Minimalist	90 - 100	Within terraces	0 - 10

Average with pool	60 - 80	5 - 10	20 - 30
Keen gardener – no pool	30 - 40	10 - 20	45 - 50

2. Take this further by using ground cover plants (See section D Appendix 4), close plantings and other forms of mulching to ensure that almost no bare soil is exposed to the sun's rays. This will reduce water losses by evaporation. Mulching is discussed in more detail later, in section 4.7.

3. Understand the climate of your garden site and the climatic needs of the types of plants you might plant. There are three levels of climate that will affect the success you have with your garden; namely the macro, micro and nano climates.

The **macro climate** is the general pattern and extremes of annual and seasonal hours of sunshine, temperatures, wind frequency and strengths, humidity, rain, frost, hail and snow in the area in which you have purchased, or might purchase a property. It is wise to investigate this before making a purchase as tourist boards and property agents tend to publish average statistics and not the extremes which are important to gardeners.

The **micro climate** is the unique climate within the boundary of your property which can become very different from even neighbouring properties. It is the extent, pattern and balance of sunshine, shade, protection from hot and cold winds, and beneficial wildlife achieved as the result of the design construction and maintenance practices of your garden.

The **nano climate**, or very localised conditions above and below ground, relating to and affecting individual or co-planted plants at various spots in your existing or planned garden.

The first, the macroclimate, you can only impact by investigating and thinking about this before you purchase a property or by moving.

The second, the microclimate, can be totally changed by high walls hedges and boundary trees, developing the garden as a series of interconnected mini gardens, internal hedges, the balance between planted areas terraces and paths, mulching practices, water features etc..

The third, the nano climate, is the most important, in relation to each plant in respect of its overall growth and particularly its regular watering needs. This is the level of climatic conditiions most easily and speedily improved by yourself.

~ 18 ~

The table below illustrates the differences between poor and good nano climates. We first published the concept in our book 'Growing healthy vegetables in Spain' in 2006.

TYPICAL CHARACTERISTICS OF:	
POOR NANO CLIMATES	GOOD NANO CLIMATES
Above ground	**Above ground**
1. Hard solid soil surface	1. Regularly loosened or well mulched surface.
2. No shade or shelter from hot/cold winds	2. Windbreaks and natural shading
3. Watering of leaves causing fungal attacks	3. Only surface watering except for rainfall
4. No beneficial insects	4. Beneficial insects, animals and birds
5. Constant insecticide/fungicide mist.	5. Symbiotic companion plantings
Below ground	**Below ground**
1. Lacks natural nutrients	1. Natural nutrients readily available in the soil
2. Compacted solid mass stunts root development	2. Open crumbly aerated soil structure enables deep root development
3. No worms	3. Large worm population
4. Sterile and with few microbes, mostly bad	4. Full of beneficial microbes

5. Variable moisture, either dry or waterlogged	5. Constant moisture, never waterlogged
6. Roots force-fed with fast chemical fertilizers	6. Roots take what they want from the soil

The types of nano climates in various parts of the garden can significantly affect the amount of water you waste.

4. If you have an existing garden, do an immediate analysis of where you use most and least water. Examine the value to you of the thirstiest plants and decide whether you should continue with them where they are, replant them to a less dry situation or take them out.

5. Many expats moving from a temperate to a drier Mediterranean climate envisage a beautiful 365 day a year colourful, perfumed and edible Garden of Eden or Shangri – La. A utopia garden with the thick shrubberies of subtropical shrubs and climbers like those that surrounded the hotel and pool areas of far east and Caribbean holiday hotels stayed in before they invested in a Mediterranean climate holiday or retirement property. Unfortunately they don't realize that very little of the Mediterranean coastline approaches subtropical conditions in summer or winter and especially in regard to the potential water needs. So do consider and realize that the water needs of the various types of gardens possible in dry areas and dry periods of weather vary enormously. The following table illustrates this vividly.

Type of garden	Examples of possible garden designs.
Thirsty	1. The English garden – reconstruction of what was left behind or still exists in England if only part time resident in Mediterranean areas
	2. The water garden – with areas for bog plants
	3. Spring/early summer annual displays – sometimes adopted by seasonal residents
	4. Botanical garden with world-wide collection of plants – some thirsty
	5. Subtropical and tropical collections of plants – all above average thirstiness

	6. Tropical fruit grown against a south facing wall – need damp soil and humidity
	7. South facing hillside garden – constant drying sun and hot southerly winds
	8. Container garden – especially if unsealed terracotta pots used
	9. Lawned gardens – especially if fine grass varieties used
	10. Wind swept gardens – especially if on ridge with winds from all directions
	11. Patio or courtyard garden if heavily planted – can get hot, window boxes and wall pots dry out regularly, even daily if annual used
	12. Soft fruit bushes and plants – mulching essential even then
Moderate water needs.	1. Botanical garden with national collection of plants – reduced needs as matures
	2. Indigenous and long naturalized plants only – Provided deep roots encouraged and no/little water when mature
	3. Vegetable gardens – a balance between summer thirst and non-thirsty winter
	4. Fruit trees – as with vegetables when young, less water as mature
	5. Arab style series of mini gardens – each with contrasting design and plantings
	6. Evergreen garden – only evergreen plants and use of dappled shade
	7. West and east facing gardens - reduced sunny hours
	8. Raised bed gardens - provided 50 to 100 cm deep beds with good soil mix
	9. Bulb garden – needs water to maintain bulbs year after year and long lasting displays
	10. Salvia collections – over 800 varieties to choose from, but few drought resistant
	11. Stone fruit trees – individual specimens and orchards
	12. Dapple shaded copse garden – with 200 to 300 planted pots.
Low water needs	1. Chinese/Japanese raked stone chipping/sand gardens – no plants!
	2. Mock dry river bed – total or an area of garden

	3. Cacti or succulent garden – plant small plants and encourage formation of deep roots, could develop as a mock dessert or sand dune garden 4. Rockeries – provided plenty of big rocks with deep small rock/chipping/volcanic mulching are used 5. Only highly drought resistant plants - only watered while they are establishing themselves 6. The minimalist contemporary garden – very few if any plants; rocks in wire cage shrub substitutes; ornaments and sculptures for interest; artificial turf areas 7. Small area of flower beds – large terraces and wide paths, gravel areas 8. Thickly mulched gardens – flower, fruit and vegetable areas – See section 4.7 9. Perennial herb gardens – mulched with stone chippings or crushed volcanic lava 10. Rose garden – provided very deep roots, perhaps self-propagated from long cuttings and thickly mulched with horse manure or alternatives – See section 4.7 11. Wooded gardens – planted with locally compatible shade loving plants 12. Olive grove – but restricted crop without any rain or watering during a six month winter/spring or summer/autumn drought 13. Natural herb shrub and tree covered hillside – kept undisturbed 14. North facing hillside gardens – lose sun early, develop natural springs 15. Wild untamed mountainsides – maintain as much as possible 16. Gardens below slopes or slabs of solid rock from which rainfall runs down onto the land below – our olive grove is watered this way - if it rains!!

6. Allow no rainwater to run off your land onto adjacent properties by building boundary walls and adjusting the slope of your land. See Section 5.2.

7. Have no plants. Probably boring but could use a collection of sculptures is in place of plants in a contemporary garden. See section 4.*16 Interesting features that don't require water.*

8. Have wire boxes of various shapes and sizes filled with rocks of various colours shapes and dimensions as a substitute for live plants and as a form of architecture or sculpture. Can make an impact, but not for most of us.

9. Plan a garden around indigenous native or long naturalised plants rather than plants from wetter or cooler areas of the world. Work with, rather than against, nature.

10. Sow or plant only drought resistant and deep rooted plants bushes and trees that need less water than thirsty shallow rooted plants. See Section 4.2. 11. If you insist on having both thirsty and drought resistant plants don't co-plant them but group plants by water needs. Co-planting not only uses more water but also stimulates attacks by moisture loving insects and fungal spores.

11. Minimise the planting of annuals in dry locations, especially in Mediterranean climate areas.

12. Plant most new plants, including bushes and trees, after autumn rains, so that roots become established before the following spring and therefore need less watering than spring plantings.

13. Plant close to the edge of hard surfaced terraces and paths so that roots go under them to find cool damp soil. Similar effects can be created by edging soft surfaced terraces and paths with rocks or terracotta edging tiles.

14. Have no lawn or at least reduce its size. See section 4.11. If you have a lawn use the thick bouncy coarser more drought resistant grass varieties that still look good when cut longer than fine varieties. The Gramma grass variety can be planted with plantlets which require less watering to establish themselves than starting with seed. There is more about lawns In Section 4.11.

15. Use areas of artificial turf instead of natural grass.

16. Develop a wild flower meadow which flowers in the Spring, instead of a lawn, by encouraging existing local plants to seed and thickening the natural flowering plant population by sowing wild plant seeds. For Spain and other parts of the Mediterranean Semillas Silvestres based in Cordoba can supply seed mixes for various types of soil and heights above sea level. Pictorial Meadows of Sheffield England became well known when they supplied the seed mixes for the colourful meadow areas of the London Olympic Park. They also provided the seed mix used to restyle the labyrinth of the Marnes Iris Garden in Spain during 2012. I am sure that there are similar suppliers in other parts of the world who have special mixes for dry gardens.

17. Establish beds for flowers fruit or vegetables between the house walls and pathways so they are watered by rain running off the eaves. By planting lantanas here you will not only save water but also deter mosquitoes.

18. If you have only shallow soil over bed rock construct raised beds with a 40 to 100 cm depth of growing medium. Raised beds can be anything from 60 cms square in size to even a hundred metres long and a 1.5 metres wide.

19. Rockeries make interesting features and require little watering if correctly constructed with plant roots buried below rocks with volcanic ash chipping mulches between rocks.

20. On rocky land fill in holes between large rocks with soil and plant drought resistant bulbs, succulents, aloes, agaves, and cacti. See useful varieties in Appendix 4.

21. Create a concrete desert or volcanic landscape with thirty centimetre diameter planting holes for plants such as cacti, aloe, agaves and succulents. Slope the concrete so that water runs to the holes.

22. If you have a high up, rarely visited or seen, window use plastic geraniums or other artificial plants or flowers rather than see dead plants most of the time. At Christmas time good quality plastic poinsettias can look great.

23. If you are an absentee gardener, only using your property for a few weeks a year, have the major plantings on the north side of the house.

24. Have no garden ponds, although they would be a sad loss. With summer floating plant cover they lose less water per square metre surface area than swimming pools.

25. If you have ponds locate them so that they are not in full sun all day.

26. Ensure that marsh plants in pots around the side of ponds do not establish roots in the soil around the pond and form a continuity of soil over the rim of the pond ,as in dry weather this can set up a natural siphoning system and result in significant losses of water.

27. In hot situations locate greenhouses in the shade of the west side of the house or in the dappled shade of tree, otherwise they can soon get to a hundred degrees even in winter.

28. Re-commission or sink wells on your property or as a local joint project with neighbours. However when purchasing a rural property check that you will own the water extraction rights.

Unfortunately some gardeners have found out too late that the water mining rights are owned by a water bottling plant.

29. If you have financial constraints or shortages of summer water, phase the development and planting up your garden to ensure that at no time will you lose plants by not being able to water them sufficiently, prior to weaning them off regular watering. When first phase plants start to mature and can be weaned off regular watering you can proceed to phase two plantings etc..

30. Shade is always important. If you take over a garden with trees fell them at your peril. Their part day semi shade could have reduced the watering needs of many plants especially those growing under the drip line. If you are designing a new garden double the number of trees you initially thought of planting. See section 4.8.

31. Take steps to collect and store as much rain water as possible and distribute it effectively. These important issues are expanded on in Section 5.1.

4.2 Select plants that require least water

1. Concentrate on varieties that enjoy a Mediterranean garden climate and are therefore highly or at least moderately drought tolerant and for inland frost pockets ones that are frost resistant as well. These characteristics are highlighted in the plant lists and descriptions included in 'Your Garden in Spain – From planning to planting and maintenance' and a summary list is attached as Appendix 4. Appendix 5 lists the wild indigenous plants that grew on our initially wild plot and the abandoned agricultural terraces that surrounded the plot awaiting inevitable development.

2. Recognise that many of the most drought resistant plants do not have large bright green soft flat smooth leaves but have adapted to cope with long hours of hot bright summer daylight. Many have narrow pointed, tough or rough textured, shiny, grey green in colour, furry or hairy leaves. Others have leaves only half way up the stems towards the flowers and some drop leaves in the summer or do not produce flowers during the hottest months. Further others die back after a spring flowering and do not start to grow up again until the late autumn or spring while other plants grow and flower all summer but the flowers only open up in the cool of the evening.

3. Then of course there are plants that store water such as cacti succulents aloes agaves and bulbs.

4. Many drought resistant plants, especially shrubs and trees put down deep tap roots. So buy these and coach them to quickly develop these roots by planting in friable soils and deep watering.

5. If you decide to have plants from other areas, recognize their preferred temperature ranges and humidities. It is interesting that the managed Madrid Royal Botanical Garden maintains the following microclimates in the desert region, subtropical and tropical greenhouses.

Desert region plants;

Summer temperatures 30 – 35 centigrade, winter temperatures 3 -5, humidity 65%.

Humid subtropical:

Summer temperatures 30 -32 centigrade, winter temperatures 10 -12, humidity 75%.

Tropical:

Summer temperatures 28 – 30 centigrade, winter temperatures 13 – 15, humidity ????

6. Aim to develop a maturing garden over the years without a constant annual change of plants and layouts based on the latest importation of plants in local garden centres or latest launches at gardening shows such as The Chelsea Flower Show. New plants inevitably need more water than mature well established ones and garden centres often don't expect boutique plants such as exotic amazon basin flowering trees to survive a winter's frosts. But there are gardeners prepared to pay hundreds of euros a year to impress summer luncheon or house quests.

7. Buy small plants with a freely growing root system, rather than large plants that are root bound in smallish pots for the size of plant.

8. Buy plants that are growing in a good compost mix that does not dry out quickly. If you don't, it can be difficult, especially if only ground palm fibres are used in the pots, to prevent an air ring developing around the pot compost and the surrounding soil after planting, due to the different drying characteristics. An immediate surface mulching can help. Interestingly plants purchased from fellow members of gardening clubs at their monthly meetings are normally prepared in good compost mixes and have high survival rates.

9. Grow plants from cuttings planted where you want the final plant or propagate in pots and plant out young when the tap root is developing fast. Use deep pots for developing cuttings with deep roots.

10. Seek out seeds for drought resistant plants. Most of the varieties found in comprehensive seed catalogues such Chiltern Seeds, Semillas Silvestres and the Mediterranean Gardening Society members seed list will not be found as plants in most garden centres. Within Spain there is, to the best of our knowledge, only one nursery, Cultidelta in Delta Ebro in southern Cataluña, offering a wide range of indigenous plants. This situation will obviously vary from country to country.

11. In the hottest spots in the garden plant only drought resistant ones. If you are tempted by thirstier subtropical plants plant them in an area of deep moisture retaining soil, and mulch with compost covered with woven or solid plastic sheeting followed by a thick layer of large rocks to shade the surface soil and roots.

12. Adapt the garden around plants that appear unexpectedly having grown from seeds dropped by birds. This way we have gained several unexpected trees including an old variety of plum tree which we have never watered, several woodland shrubs and a useful patch of acanthus that grow through pruned back lantanas in the spri, before becoming covered by the lantanas until next year. Most importantly they germinated and survived because the growing conditions were perfect and they didn't need watering.

13. Let plants that appear unexpectedly as a result of self-seeding grow where they are. They will have found a perfect spot and often need no watering while a purchased plant will. We have recent experience of this with both echium candicans and echium pininama plants

14. Plant if possible after the autumn rains so that roots have up to six to eight months to establish themselves before dangerous drought conditions return in the spring and summer.

15. It is a pity from the point of view of creating a low water needs garden that some popular drought resistant plants such as agaves, yucca, acacias and lantanas are being included in lists for possible eradication in gardens and garden centres as well as in the countryside in case they become a danger to rare indigenous species in the event of further global warming.

16. If you purchase plants from specialist nurseries in less dry areas to that of your garden recognize that they will need to adapt to a new soil and microclimate.

4.3 Soil improvement

1. Unfortunately many plants are in a permanent state of stress and survival due to a combination of poor soil and poor watering.

2. Improve soils and composts before planting anything, particularly in terms of fertility and water absorption and holding capacity

3. The overall purpose of improving soils and composts is to:

- Ensure that the roots of plants can develop rapidly and healthily to extract moisture and nutrients and give plants stability as they grow tall and heavy.
- Assist plants to develop deep roots as soon as possible.
- Increase and maintain nutrient levels.
- Increase and maintain populations of beneficial microorganisms.
- Reduce the number of unwanted microbes and wildlife.
- Increase and maintain moisture retaining properties while maintaining free draining properties except for moisture loving plants such as marsh plants around ponds.

4. Recognise the nutrient needs of plants and the risk of adding too much nitrogen to the soil which can result in an unnatural rapid growth of plants which can be too sappy and attract insects and fungal attack, as well as being unnecessarily structurally weak and require staking. Naturally this rapid growth will require an unnatural amount of water.

The main nutrient needs of garden plants will be, as in nature, as follows.
Water – Help roots extract nutrients from the soil, enable plant cell strength and rigidity. Unfortunately much of the water irrigated in gardens is not available to the roots for long or long enough.
Phosphorus – Development of strong root structures.
Potassium – Development of flower buds, flowers, seed heads, fruit and drought disease resistance.
Nitrogen – Development of plant structure – roots, stems, branches and leaves.
Carbon dioxide – Taken in at night through leaves and converted to organic molecules to build plant tissues and store energy.
Vitamin H – Helps carbon dioxide transfer in photosynthesis.
Vitamin P types – Aids pigmentation and nitrogen fixation from air.
Carbon – Aids photosynthesis.

Magnesium – Aids chlorophyll formation and maintenance of green pigmentation of plants.

Sodium – Aids photosynthesis in some plants.

Vitamin K types – Energy transfer in photosynthesis.

Vitamin E – Protects chloroplasts from oxidation.

Calcium – Cell growth and rigidity plus resistance to disease

Boron – Aids development of cell structures and natural disease control.

Oxygen – To oxidize and extract energy from organic food molecules.

Sulphur – Aids general plant and soil health, enhances extraction of minerals and when dusted on surface of leaves prevents fungal diseases.

Iron – Helps chlorophyll creation and the prevention of bleaching of leaves.

Zinc, manganese – Prevent yellowing of leaves.

Iodine – stimulates growth of some plants.

Copper, molybdenum – Essential micro nutrients.

Vitamins A, B, C, D – Aid seed germination of some plants.
Vitamin

Microbes – When in soil help convert nutrients in soils/composts into more easily extractable forms.

Fibre – Improves structure and water retention of soil.

Ensuring that the nutrients are in the soil and that moisture surrounds all the roots of plants to enable them to extract the essential nutrients continuously is an essential gardening skill.

5. Interestingly, as I explain in the book *'Living well from our garden – Mediterranean style'*, the same nutrients are required by the human body for healthy growth and living. It therefore not surprising that urine, neat or diluted, was and still is a very effective natural fertilizer for many plants, and neat you don't need water. At one of our talks a couple of years ago an elderly lady commented that she had a garden of just 200 containers and, confirmed by others at the talk, she had the best garden in the neighbourhood. She added that, just as her grandmother and mother had done, all pots were fertilised and watered with diluted night waters. Likewise when gardening I regularly feed a scented leaf pelargonium plant. Today in May it is 1.7 metres tall and has a spread of 2.3 metres.

6. If you have purchased a house, or are building a house, on land that was originally agricultural you have inherited large old trees you may have struck a gold mine of nutrients if

donkeys, mules and horses had been tethered to them in the shade for many decades or even centuries. Two lucky friends realised that the soil under a several hundred year old oak tree looked very dark coloured and rich and enormous weeds were growing there. Within a year they had a very productive vegetable plot growing around the tree with the gems being giant squash plants especially a pilgrim's gourd, Curbita leucantia/Lagenaria sicerania. This just took off and reached the upper branches of the tree, well above the height of a two storey house. When I was asked to visit to see the amazing plant and produce large size gourds hung from the highest branches like colourful decorations on a giant Christmas tree. The soil was obviously nutrient rich and did not dry out quickly.

Few readers are likely to be so lucky but may well have an old carob tree on their land. If so dig out the rich black compost under the tree and use it to enrich and improve the moisture holding capacity of soils and composts.

7. Since drought resistant plants generally have deep tap roots it is important that soil is loosened and improved to a depth of 30 to 50 centimetres when planting new plants, depending on whether you are planting relatively small plants, shrubs or trees.

8. Don't walk on cultivated ground as this consolidates dry Mediterranean clayey soils and after a time it is difficult to change the soil back to a friable open structure. It is interesting that after forest and mountainside fires in Spain one rediscovers long lost paths and find that they have been largely clear of plants although hidden by growth from the plants growing either side of the paths.

9. In general aim for a 20 to 40% organic material content, the former for succulents and the latter for vegetables.

10. A soil improvement gel based product such as the internationally known TerraCottem can reduce water needs by 50 to 70%. See www.terracottem.com for full information. Apparently their most important market world-wide is now the planting of shrubs and trees. For the past twelve years we have used the product extensively to help establish plants, including flowering shrubs and trees more rapidly and make it easier to grow summer vegetable crops and establish fruit trees with the minimum of watering. Your nearest distributor can be obtained by emailing info@terravida.com in Spain or info@terracottem.com for the international office.

11. Only improve the areas of the garden which you plan to plant up to ensure that the benefit of available manures composts and TerraCottem is maximised. Try and used compost heap

manures, the black compost from rotted leaves under mature trees, dried or well-rotted horse goat or sheep manures. If you have to use poultry manures use it sparingly as it is strong. If you have a rabbit or two their droppings are also useful.

12. Sacks of worm compost are increasingly available and are a very useful additive for both soils and composts, especially for containers and raised beds used to grow vegetables.

13. Increase the worm population of your garden by:

a. Breeding them in your compost heap. This can be stimulated by placing the compost heap on soil with no plastic or concrete base, keeping the compost heap damp but not wet, adding layers of damp newspaper every 30 centimetres when you fill the compost heap.

b. Finding a pile of several year old well-rotted goat or sheep manure full of red worms and negotiate to buy a few bags or even a lorry load.

c. Buy a kilo or two from a worm breeder.

d. Buy a home wormery for composting green kitchen waste.

Suppliers of worms and wormeries can be found on the internet. For Europe try www.wiggly wigglers.co.uk as a starter.

14. If you are starting a new garden it is worth buying a lorry load of compost from a council or commercial run Eco-park composting unit that composts an areas garden waste if one exists within a reasonable distance from your home.

15. Recognise that many Mediterranean coastal mountains are green all the year round with plants growing in the gaps between rocks where organic material has gathered and decomposed for millions of years. Their roots find moisture and nutrients below the rocks even in summer, so don't remove all the stones, rocks and decaying leaves from gardens as these help to maintain moisture levels and cool protective areas for delicate roots.

16. A sprinkling of sulphur powder can help increase the acidity of soil and kill off insects such as leather jackets and ants, plus unwanted microbes. This can help maintain the water absorption and retention capacity of soils.

17. Add sand or fine grit to heavy clay soils to improve their friability. This helps improve and maintain the oxygen content and free draining qualities. Cacti, succulents and perennial herbs will benefit from the addition of grit or coarse crushed volcanic lava.

18. Less watering and a sprinkling of dried neem powder can help get rid of slugs and harmful microbes. If you can't trace neem powder, often it is in blocks, locally contact kontakt@niem-handel.de who understand English. The product is very light so postal changes should be economic.

4.4 Preparing planting areas and planting holes

1. The effectiveness of your approach to planting up new plants is critical to their speed of root establishment, achieving their planned contribution to your garden, reaching maturity and surviving for many years.

2. If you are planning a bed for a dense population of various types of plants improve the soil in the total area before planting anything down to a depth of thirty to fifty centimetres, depending on what you intend to plant.

3. If the soil is pre-improved as above, make planting holes the same size as the pot in which the plant comes. Work a little TerraCottem gel into the base of the hole and then plant and firm the soil around the plant.

4. If you plan to plant a drought resistant hedge such as cupressus or oleander recognise that it will be a few years before the roots are sufficiently deep for you to wean the hedge off watering. So first dig a trench the length of your planned hedge fifty centimetres deep and forty centimetres wide. Then fill the bottom half of the trench with a twenty percent manure soil mix with some TerraCottem worked in. Incidentally, we did not know of this product for the first fifteen years in Spain but now we always keep a box available and recommend the product to friends and others whom we might be coaching in the practical techniques of Mediterranean gardening.

Firm the mix and then plant the hedging plants using a similar mix to fill the trench. Finally, saturate the soil in the trench. Keep the soil damp for two or three years then stop watering to test whether the hedge is now established sufficiently to survive without watering.

5. When planting individual perennial plants shrubs and trees in unprepared or long unused areas first dig a planting hole twice to three or four times the width and depth of the pot in which the plant comes. Loosen the bottom soil and fill the hole with water and allow to drain and then repeat. Then infill to the depth of the roots of the plant with a friable compost, /manure soil mix, again with some TerraCottem added in, to create a dampness reservoir to attract roots downwards in dry weather. Then plant, spreading the roots out and infill with a good compost soil mix firming as you go.

6. Wherever and whatever you plant the aim is to provide growing conditions as near as possible to those found in areas where similar types of plants are growing successfully in the wild. Look around when you walk in the countryside especially at what is growing on shady and sunny sides of tracks in the spring and autumn. Often many young seedlings in the sunny areas in the spring will have not survived the summer due to baked shallow and consolidated soil conditions, while those in cooler shady areas will have started to grow well.

7. Some plants such as perennial herbs do not like being planted in clayey soils, even if improved, so aim to grow on rockeries, above dry stone walls, in ridges into which plenty of grit small rocks or stones have been mixed or in holes on level ground where twenty percent of stones and grit have been added to the infill soil and compost mix. In the late 80's, the early days of our garden, we attempted to establish an Elizabethan knot style herb bed in a red clay soil using plantlets from fields abandoned awaiting an urbanization. It was a total disaster as we discovered that different herbs needed a different soil compost and grit mix. But the soil mix we arrived at was perfect for growing lavender which has only been replaced once in over twenty years when plants became very woody.

8. When planting in very stony or rocky areas we suggest you sink a plastic plant pot three times the diameter of the one in which the plant was purchased and two to three times the depth. Then replant your plant in the newly buried pot using a good quality soil mix, In this way water will not be lost sideways and the roots will be encouraged to go deep rather than sideways.

9. If you want to plant large shrubs or trees in similar stony or rocky areas, or in areas you wish to infill with rocks or builders rubble, do similar to the above using inexpensive plastic dustbins

or discarded plastic barrels that one sometimes sees in the rubbish bins on industrial estates or in agricultural areas. Just cut out a drainage hole out of the bottom before you fill them with a water retentive soil/compost mix, say 70 percent soil 20 percent compost and 10 percent composted manure. This is a useful way of planting trees and shrubs in the sloping infill surrounding a raised up swimming pool or if infilling a natural gully.

10. Plant things as deep as possible, but bear in mind the susceptibility to fungi and rotting off of some plants. Also avoid burying the graft on fruit trees, roses and some vegetable plants such as melons and aubergines. The graft is best kept five to ten centimetres above the soil.

11. In our terraced garden there are many exposed or shallowly buried rocks from carrying and moveable sizes, to boulders of several square metres surface area. Some we found by digging around and knocking in iron rods before planting in the early years. Where we knew of the rocks we dug planting holes to the side of the rocks so that plants had unrestricted passage downwards for their roots.

In some cases we inevitably planted above large rocks some fifteen centimetres below the depth of our planting holes. As a result we have a few stunted permanent bonsais and some trees that took many years to grow until their roots had found a way across and down under the rock where moisture lay. But this is the diversity, interest and fun of dry gardening which involves getting to understand the limits of nature. It's very different to gardening on a piece of Mediterranean agricultural land with a garden that can be totally flooded each week in the summer from surrounding agricultural water channels or a walled garden in Kuwait ,where water is free, that can be flooded every couple of days to maintain a garden as green and colourful as a tropical jungle.

12. Some years ago Clodagh, my wife, looked after a 5000 square metre garden with strict instructions from the owners not to use the irrigation system unless absolutely necessary, so most plants in the garden were small but healthy. Then one year she had a call from the owners asking 'What have you done? The plants along the south side of the house are double to triple the size and bursting with flowers? We hate to see the watering bill'. Clodagh calmly suggested that the owner went upstairs and looked out from a terrace at the neighbours garden. It had been landscaped by raising up the land a couple of metres and then planted up with giant sub - tropical plants. They were being kept alive with a river of water gushing out of a fully open irrigation system. Much water ran under a recently planted hedge and into the previously dry

shrub beds that Clodagh tended. Her client never had to use his own watering system again! But it was no longer waterless gardening, albeit at someone else's expense!

13. The 5000 square metre Kensington Roof Garden in London, now on top of a Richard Branson office block, was developed in the 1930's with 1.5 metre deep soil and today has some 75 full-size trees and a deep running stream. However few buildings, especially residential houses and apartment blocks are now constructed with the necessary loadbearing capacity for even 200 square metre gardens or a collection of trees and shrubs in large containers. However, new technology has enable gardens with mature trees to be grown in just ten to twenty centimetres of growing medium sandwiched between an impermeable membrane covered with a thin draining substrate and a surface mulching membrane. The watering needs in relation to the extent of roof gardens can therefore now be remarkably low.

4.5 Watering

1. Recognise that there are six types of watering available – natural morning dews, rainfall, hand watering with a watering can, watering with a hose, irrigation systems and flooding from a channeled agricultural water supply system.

We suggest you maximise the benefit of the first two and minimise the long term need for the last two to develop deep roots and reduce watering needs to a minimum.

2. Water late evening and during the night when soils are cooling down and will better absorb and retain water.

3. Allow plants to show first signs of stress, droopy leaves and flower stalks plus falling fruit, before watering to stimulate deeper roots

4. Aim to water the deeper roots and the soil beneath them to stimulate deeper and stronger root balls rather than upward growing and surface roots. Test how well you are doing by digging a few holes alongside plants to test the dampness of the soil at various depths and then infilling and giving the replaced soil a good soaking.

5. An easy way to get water down to deep roots is to sink lengths of 5 centimetre diameter plastic water tubing alongside plants and water through these with a hose or watering can. If planting large trees commercial underground watering systems can be purchased and installed.

6. A once or twice a week deep watering is preferable for most plants than a daily or every other day shallow watering. If you have an irrigation system with a timer it is best, except for annuals, to water for 30 minutes once a day for small young shallow rooted plants than twice a day for fifteen minutes, and thirty to sixty minutes twice a week than half that time four times a week for deeper rooted plants like trees for instance.

7. Once deep roots start to develop wean plants off water other than natural rainfalls, to the stage where you can stop watering. We cannot believe the number of gardens with irrigation systems that still water things, such as irises and fig trees, 365 days a year twenty years after they were planted.

8. Don't water long established plants even when you have drought conditions unless they show serious signs of stress. We have been amazed during this year's six months of drought how some trees have grown more than normal and have had abnormally good crops of fruit. The drought obviously prompted already deep roots to go even deeper.

9. Identify areas where some of your saved water could, with benefit, be allocated for use elsewhere. For instance use more water to get new plants off to a good start by deeper, more thorough watering. This can speed the establishment of strong deep root systems so that watering can be cut back and indeed ceased after a couple of years.

10. If you install a permanent automatic time controlled irrigation system establish seasonal patterns of watering and use adjustable drip feeds to each plant. Turn off or remove redundant drips as the garden matures.

11. In a large or complex garden install a sectional watering system with a timer that can water each section at different time intervals and durations.

12. Turn off irrigation systems for a few days or even weeks after heavy rainfalls.

13. Use perforated or woven irrigation tubing rather than jets or sprays alongside lines of vegetables.

14. Check irrigation systems weekly to ensure that there are no expensive leaks .

15. Check and clean jets once or twice a year so that the system can be effective at a lower pressure and therefore use less water through the cleared jets. Install a filter before the timer

on irrigation systems to take out small particles of grit in the town's water supply that could block jets.

16. For shrubs and trees water on the drip line and just beyond where searching roots will start to congregate rather than round the trunk which could stunt sideways root growth and cause trunks to rot.

17. Get water down to the roots of young flowering and evergreen treesand fruit trees by burying one or two lengths of five or ten centimetre diameter plastic tubing long enough to reach the lowest roots and water through the tube. Commercial wide bore underground watering systems are available to use with recently planted giant mature trees.

18. Reduce the extent of watering midsummer hibernating plants such as gazanias to just keep them alive. No amount of water will get them back into flower before the weather cools.

19. Keep pot and container grown plants that are not totally drought resistant in semi or dappled shade rather than full sun.

20. Use containers, including window boxes, with built in water reservoirs.

21. Inexpensive reservoirs can be established on window boxes sited behind security bars by sitting a five litre bottle on the end with a drip feed head attached to a short length of five millimetre irrigation tubing pushed through a small hole into the water bottle, just above its base. You can adjust the flow to just what is required to keep plants healthy. One can also buy drip heads that screw onto the top of one and a half litre bottles.

22. Mix in TerraCottem water retaining gel type soil improvers to reduce watering by 50% to 75%. See www.terracottem.com.

23. While discussing technological solutions have a look at www.viaqua.com. We believe that we have had benefits from using Vi-Aqua's water electrolysis technology over the past ten years in both the flower and flower gardens. The main benefits for waterless gardeners are stronger root systems and more green growth per litre of water.

24. Finally something more down to earth. Don't waste water used to wash fruit and vegetables, steam or boil vegetables or water from humidifier units. Each can be used

conveniently to water plants in containers. Patricia Philson reported that she keeps a 5 litre plastic bottle in the kitchen to collect such waters and also adds left over tea infusions.

25. Swimming pool back wash water can be used for tough shrubs and trees provided it does not have a high salt or residual chlorine content.

4.6 Reducing evaporation losses

Evaporation losses can be enormous in hot and windy weather for two reasons. Firstly if exposed directly to the hot sun the top surface layer of soils and composts dry out fast and become crusty rock like, especially in red clay soils. Secondly as this dryness goes deeper and deeper minute diameter capillary tubes form from the lower levels to the surface. These allow moisture to evaporate out through the surface pores and one can end up with rock hard soil with just a minimal residual moisture level locked up in clay cells, that becomes not available to roots. Fortunately, as outlined below, there are a good number of practical actions that can be taken.

1. Close planting so that the soil is always shaded. When first planting up a garden, it is wise to plant some temporary sacrificial plants between the initially small permanent plants. Recognise that these will be eventually smothered and probably killed as the permanent plants spread and mature.

2. Hoeing between plants reduces the chance of capillary tubes forming permanently but it does also create a new layer of aerated soil that dries quickly. The best solution is to use a form of mulching such as bark, stone chippings, leaves and ground lava as discussed fully in the next section, section 4.7 .

3. Maximise mulching opportunities to retain moisture and recycle nutrients; mulching being the process of allowing or placing a protective layer of shading and moisture retaining materials or substances over the soil surrounding plants of all sorts.

4. Even more fundamental to the first three ideas is the need to ensure that soil and compost mixes are friable and water retentive. As mentioned earlier adding a water retaining gel such as TerraCottem can help. Apologies for mentioning this product several times but it does work and can be an invaluable plant saver for gardeners new to hot dry climates and absentee gardeners who are only resident for three to six months a year. Interestingly TerraCottem is now widely used in Australia for shrub and tree plantings.

5. Locate window boxes on the north east and west facing windowsills balconies and terraces rather than the hottest south facing ones. Naturally swop round the north and south if you live in the southern hemisphere.

6. Grow summer leaf vegetables in a shady or half shady beds, raised beds, growing tables or containers, or fix up a woven shade to use in the summer.

7. Install blinds or awnings on balconies and terraces to protect plants in containers from the hottest suns.

8. Use glazed terracotta pots and containers, or ones made from other non porous materials.

9. If untreated terracotta ones are your choice for their appearance, line them with a plastic pot plastic bag or sheeting; or paint the inside with a water proofing paint or solution.

10. Have light coloured tiled, rock slab or stone chipping terraces around pools. Dark black granite for instance gets so hot that upward thermal heat currents form increasing evaporation from a pool in the middle and from plants and the compost in containers.

11. Cover pools and Jacuzzis when not in use.

12. Locate pools and Jacuzzis where they are not in full sun all day to prevent the surface of the water from superheating to reduce the daytime evaporation rate.

13. Water plants in the cool of the evening, or the first half of the night, rather than in the morning or at midday.

14. Water deeply to get down to the main tap roots rather than only shallowly wetting the minor shallow roots that can turn up to the surface and soon dry out in hot weather. This was discussed in detail in section 4.5.

15. Plant trees for shade from the sun and as windbreaks. See Apendix 4 for ideas of suitable varieties.

16. Plant shrubs as internal windbreaks to protect smaller plants.

17. Locate plants in containers in the semi or dappled shade or in situations that only receive direct sunlight for part of the day.

18. Grow summer leaf vegetables under shading in hot locations.

19. Install blinds and awnings on open and closed terraces to shade plants from both high summer and low winter suns.

20. Set up temporary summer shading over vulnerable newly planted plants and broad leaved autumn flowering sages.

4.7 Mulch more and more

Mulching is important in Mediterranean and other dry climate gardens as it is an easy and often inexpensive way of preventing water evaporation losses and can be the life saver of thirstier plantings during the hot summer months.

For practical purposes **mulching** is the practice and process of covering the soil or compost mixes under and around plants with ground cover materials that primarily keep the surface of the soil moist and reduce the chance of weeds growing , but there are in fact a number of other important benefits as listed below. A description of numerous mulching methods will then follow on.

Benefits of mulching

- Prevents the surface of the soil from drying out and baking hard.

- Prevents the formation of minute capillary tubes in hard baked soils through which moisture evaporates from lower levels.

- Invisible transportation of rain water under chippings laid over solid plastic sheeting.

- Reduces the chance of soil compacting which destroys the essential space between soil particles which fill with moisture and oxygen in healthy soils.

- Keeps roots cool in hot weather.

- Protects roots from frost damage during cold winter spells.

- Reduces chance of weeds germinating and growing.

- Helps keep areas tidy and attractive.

- Organic mulches, like compost from a compost heap, recycle growth nutrients to the soil.

- Can hide irrigation tubing.

The following are some of the mulching ideas we have used, separately or in combination, plus a couple of things we would like to try if we could source the materials inexpensively.

1. Create a living carpet mulch by planting trailing and cascading plants between perennials and shrubs to prevent any drying sunlight to reach the surface of the soil. In one area of our garden we have allowed a carpet of wild strawberries and their dead leaves to develop as a thick mulch. Drying leaves provide an early warning that the soil is drying out in mid-summer.

2. Mulch along rows of raspberry canes and other soft fruit bushes with layers of comfrey leaves, compost from the compost heap, pine needles and grass cuttings from your or a neighbour's lawn that has not been treated recently with any chemical products.

3. Surround plants and shrubs with small weathered rocks on the rockery and with small rocks over breathable plastic sheeting in shrub/flower beds and on top of the compost in containers.

4. Place stone slabs or large rocks over the roots of climbing plants.

5. When planting trees place rock slabs over the planted roots five centimetres below the final soil level and then cover with soil.

6. Plant around the edge of large immovable rocks so that the roots grow under the rock seeking cool moisture.

7. Lay stone chippings over breathable plastic membrane between trees.

8. Lay areas of stone chippings over solid plastic sheeting to move rain water from areas where it is not need to others where it can be absorbed around plants.

9. Lay solid stone paths around planted areas and plant small plants close to the path so that they develop long roots that grow under the path to extract stored moisture.

10. As an alternative to small rocks a thick layer of fine volcanic lava or stone chippings can be used on rockeries and to cover the compost in containers. Bark chippings are not recommended for these applications as they can blow around, don't look natural in such settings and can harbour plant eating beetles that might devour the trunks/stems of small plants. One can also use layers of broken sea shells with whole shells as the surface level.

11. Expanded clay Tufa balls can also be used for containers in sheltered situations. In very windy places they can blow around when dry.

12. Leave leaves to rot under hedges, trees and ground cover plants.

13. Plant vegetable plantlets through holes in sheets of black plastic.

14. Plant fruit trees through holes in black plastic sheeting and cover the holes with a layer of compost, small rocks, or nut shells.

15. Not yet done personally but we would like to mulch our entire fruit and nut orchard with ten to fifteen centimetres of almond or walnut shells as done by a friend in Mallorca. This mulch looks attractive and is firm to walk on. Search out the nearest nut cracking unit or a supplier of nut shells for stove heaters.

16. Also if we could find a source of broken up terracotta tiles and natural clay bricks in various colours and sizes we would incorporate these in various designs for the large gardens of several friends. In our garden, natural moss covered stones and rocks plus 1.5 cm sized stone chippings with a touch of pink suit better.

17. Add a thick layer of well-rotted compost around vegetable plants.

18. Use the browning leaves to mulch around banana plants and papaya trees. This recycles nutrients as well as reducing moisture evaporation.

19. Cover the soil with overlapping sheets of newspaper dampened with a dilute flour/water mix and cover with soil. Not only will moisture losses be reduced but worms will be attracted to breed under and within the newspaper sheets.

20. For areas of cacti or palms sand or pea shingle can provide an effective mulch.

21. Palm fronds and pine needles can provide effective mulches for areas of soft fruit.

22. Mulch strawberries and between rows of vegetables with straw.

23. Mulch the compost in containers with two layers of small pine cones or nut shells from your cracked almonds, walnuts, waste from coffee bean grinding etc..

24. If you cut trees down hire a chipping machine and use the chippings to mulch under shrubs or make paths.

25. When we take excess weeds out of our ponds we use it as a nutrient rich mulch in places where it will not be an eyesore.

26. It is not ecological but one can bury a few cut up sheets of the water absorbing plastic foam used to stuff garden seat cushions a few centimetres deep.

27. Mulch less visible areas including around fruit trees with the rejected grape skins and stems from a local winery.

28. It you live near a Neem tree plantation or oil extraction plant mulch with the rejected crushed shells.

29. If you have an undisturbed area of mountainside or woodland do not remove the many years of natural mulching between rocks and under trees. Rather plant through the natural mulch and copy in other areas of the garden. Overall the best we can do is to copy the natural mulching that has gone on for millions of years.

30. Mulch seed potatoes with a deep cover of rotting pine needles and top up several times as leaves appear. This is a productive form of mulching that produces excellent new potatoes.

31. Mulch with a thick layer of compost and then cover with a layer of cardboard from large electrical appliance boxes, then cover with more compost or stone chippings. Thank you, Sophie Green, for sending in this idea as a response to Section 7.3.

32. If you use pine bark chippings laid over woven plastic sheeting recognise that you need a 10 to 20 centimetres depth of chippings to achieve a significant water saving. Just two or five centimetres will move in strong winds leaving bare areas of plastic showing. This is neither decorative nor effective mulching.

33. Grass cuttings can be useful mulches, especially along rows of soft fruit, provided the lawns have not been recently treated with weed killers,

34. Watch out for thrown out rugs and rolls of carpets by rubbish bins. Cut them into 30 to 40 centimetre strips and lay along both sides of potato ridges after planting and also along raised ridges or humps prepared for growing courgettes and squashes. You can plant overwintering peas in the holes after harvesting and they will require little watering.

35. Consider doubling the depth of all mulches in the garden.

4.8 The importance of shade

1. Recognise that many plants do better if not in full sun all day long as they dry out more slowly, have longer flowering periods and need less frequent and less voluminous watering. For example the area of our Mediterranean garden in full sun all day long in mid- summer is only 30%. Of the remainder 30% is cyclically in full sun for half the day, 30% is permanently dappled or semi shade and 10% is deep shade all day long. Water losses in the full sun situations can be many times greater than semi or partially shaded areas both for open soil areas and containers.

2. In the book 'Apartment Gardening Mediterranean Style' we included the following general guidelines for the water needs of different types of plants in various containers in full sun and semi-shaded situations during the summer and winter.

Types of plants and weather	For thirsty plants				For drought resistant plants			
	Hot summer ***		Cool winter **		Hot summer **		Cool winter *	
Types of Containers	Full sun	Semi-shade	Full sun	Semi Shade	Full sun	Semi shade	Full sun	Semi shade
Pot – 20 cm diameter	300ml	200ml	300ml	200ml	100ml	50ml	50ml	10ml
Pot – 40 cm diameter	500ml	250ml	500ml	250ml	150ml	75ml	75ml	30ml
Window box – 10 litres	1 litre	700ml	1 litre	700ml	300ml	150ml	150ml	60ml
Tub – 40 litres	4 litres	3 litres	4 litres	3 litres	1.5 litres	750ml	750ml	300ml
Trough – 80 litres	8 litres	6 litres	8 litres	6 litres	3 litres	1.5 litres	1.5 litres	600ml

Volumes of water indicated are required: ***Every two days, **Every week, *Every two weeks

2. Do recognise that it is preferable on apartment terraces, and in the garden and on the allotment, to water plants in the evening as the sun goes down so that the water is soaked up by the compost or soil with the minimum of evaporation losses. Also recognise that many plants will grow healthier if watered with rain water rather than chlorinated tap water or water from a salt based purifier.

3. Recognise that shaded soil will retain night dew dampness longest, be cooler and therefore lose least water by evaporation during the day.

4. Recognise that shade can be provided by evergreen trees, by deciduous trees in leaf, by sunshades and sails, by blinds and awnings, by gazeboes and tunnels, by large plants for adjacent smaller plants, by woven shading material and the house and other buildings.

5. Plant tall hedges and/or trees on east and/or south boundaries to create a long shady area several metres deep on the shady side.

6. Use woven shading/windbreak material to shade vulnerable young plants ,seedlings and seedbeds. We have good crops of annual broad leaved herbs and salad leaves throughout the

summer by growing them in containers under a large umbrella and also on a grow table with a woven plastic shade attached.

7. We believe that the natural shade provided by trees and plant covered gazeboes is preferable to that provided by umbrellas and sails.

8. Plant sun sensitive plants, like large leaved bignonias, in dappled shaded areas.

9. Recognise that in hot countries annual herbs won't survive in the sun or will go to seed fast. It is better to grow them in dappled shade or on the north side of the house. We grow a pot of coriander, that is liable to go to seed fast, in the shade inside our north facing front porch.

10. Recognise the dangers of removing much of the inherited shade in a mature or overgrown abandoned garden. The following case history is interesting.

A couple we know took over a house on a terraced hillside which had not been occupied for almost ten years and the garden had not been tended or watered for that time. To say the least it was overgrown with spreading blackberry bushes, wild clematis and other wild climbers, thickets of self-seeded pine and acacia trees etc., hiding any plants that may have survived.

For over a year Clodagh, my wife, helped clear the undergrowth square metre by square metre from the front gate to the bottom of the mountainside garden, overgrown terrace by overgrown terrace. The following plants were found to be alive under the undergrowth or emerging above.

Acacia trees, agaves, aloes, aloe versa, aeoniums, bignonias, bougainvilleas, bulbs, carob trees, cipres trees, gazanias, euryops, ferns, heathers, hibiscuses, honeysuckles, jacarandas, lantanas, mandarin trees, morning glory, oleanders, pine trees, pittosporum, plumbago, rhucelia, rosemary, thyme and yuccas.

Many of the perennial plants were large enough and healthy enough to take cuttings to root up in a nursery bed until a suitable place for planting out had been cleared. Naturally some were weakened by having seen little light for some years but most soon strengthened themselves and greened up.

However problems started when the owners decided to cut down some of the surviving trees.

Some plants had survived because there was often a morning mist and dew on the hillside and they had been in dappled shade or deeper shade for some years. But once exposed to continuous sunlight they needed to be watered, so an irrigation system needed to be installed.

4.9 Protection from drying winds

1. Plant high hedges or /and spreading trees around the entire plot or an inner garden if you have a very large plot.

2. Design garden as a series of mini gardens each surrounded by high walls, hedges, shrubs or trees.

3. Use medium high plants to develop internal hedges which can give shelter to smaller plants planted close on the down-wind side.

4. Use attractive low, 15 to 30 centimetre high, woven wattle, brushwood or cane windbreak fences within the flower or vegetable garden.

5. All forms of mulching can help – see section 4.7

6. Plant young tender plants in wide holes imitating the Canary Island method of digging deep holes to plant fruit trees to get down to the rich cool damp soil below a metre or two of old larva layers and protect trees from howling gales.

7. Plant down-wind below terraces and boundary or internal walls.

8. Protect small young plants, flowers or vegetables, with a temporary half circle of rocks or the ears of Opuntia cacti. We have used the latter successfully with young melons and courgettes for instance. We first saw the practice on the island of Malta.

9. Also from Malta, surround a vegetable plot or entire garden with high Opuntia hedges.

10. Seal potted cuttings in large plastic bags to provide a constant humidity microclimate and prevent drying out.

11. Protect young plants or patches of seeds with large size empty water bottles with the bottoms cut out and a cane pushed through the pouring hole for stability. I have just covered rows of summer herb seeds on a growing table in this way.

12. Use sealed early season tunnel cloches on vegetable plot.

13. Locate poultry runs down wind of a high wall to prevent birds being blown about.

4.10 Reduce drainage losses

1. Immediately improve fast draining stony soils by working in copious amounts of moisture holding organic matter, such as compost and well rotted manures as already discussed in section 4.3.

2. Dig out areas you wish to plant up to a depth of 30 or 40 centimetres and lay a sheet of impermeable black plastic as a shallow bowl as the base. Make a few small drainage holes or slits and infill with a good soil mix as discussed in section 4.3.

3. You could go further with '2' by lining the sides and base with plastic sheeting to create a sunken trough bed.

4. Avoid planting up and watering fast draining rocky or stony areas or plant perennials shrubs and trees in sunken large pots or various sizes of dustbins and plastic barrels with part of the bottom cut out to avoid sideways water loss and reduce vertical losses.

5. In very stony or gravelly soil dig out trench beds forty centimetres deep and eighty centimetres wide and of a convenient length alongside a path, at the end of a path, along a fence or between rows of fruit trees on a sloping site. Line the trench with black plastic sheeting taking it over the top of the sides. Make two centimetre planting holes at fifty centimetre intervals and pile stones or broken pottery over them. Then fill the trenches with a good soil/compost mix. Wire down the excess plastic two centimetres below the top of the trench so that run off water can drain into the trenches.

6. Don't over water beyond what the soil or compost down to the depth of the roots can absorb.

4.11 Reduce thirsty lawn losses

1. Have no lawn.

2. Cut to leave grass twice as long as your normal practice to date.

3. Water during the relative cool of the night or just before sunset or early morning.

4. Reduce lawn in half and increase areas of paths and terraces.

5. Mix TerraCottem soil improvement gel into soil before laying turf or sowing seeds. This was done when many Mediterranean golf courses were constructed.

6. Use a course drought resistant grass such as gramma which can be planted as plantlets or sown as seed.

7. Sow an area of spring flowered meadow grass and then just strim twice a year.

8. Go a stage further by removing all the grass and sowing a small or large area of just spring flowers after improving the soils.

8. If you must have a lawn, sow or lay it after the autumn rains and not in the spring.

9. Recognise that a frequently watered and fed very short cut putting green lawn is susceptible to cat and dog circles plus weeds which come because you are always watering.

10. Use artificial turf.

11. Change to a large terrace surrounded by drought resistant shrubs or cacti, or a rockery.

12. Change to a labyrinth of paths and narrow herb beds.

13.Before early retirement, I used to initially drive down to Spain in early June and then, until mid- September, commute back to the UK by plane for ten days each month to keep my business ticking over and the garden tidy, especially the lawn. The latter was often a problem because it had grown considerably during my absence and it often rained soon after my return, so having the lawn neat and tidy before each of my return flights to Spain was often touch and go. So the lawn had to go!

Early October a large sheet of solid plastic was purchased and cut into three large circles of different sizes. These were laid over the lawn, covering it about 80% in an interesting pattern. The outer edges were then covered with circles of old bricks that matched the Georgian bricks of the house and the centres filled with pea shingle. The patches of lawn remaining were dug out and replaced by top soil before rearranging existing plants and infilling with a few new ones. There was within a weekend no lawn to cut ever again and a series of more interestingly shaped flower beds. Within a year the roots of many plants had sort out the continuous reservoir of moisture under the plastic circles and the need for summer watering was reduced.

During the next visit to Spain the same approach was used to get rid of an area of remaining rough meadow grass in the emergent Mediterranean waterless garden.

4.12 Growing fruit

The following steps can be taken to minimise the watering needs of fruit plants, bushes, vines and trees.

1.Plant the most drought resistant varieties of fruits. There is a practical selection in Appendix 4 section M.

2.Plant small sized or even dwarf varieties of fruit trees that will yield useful harvests with moderate water needs. If you plant larger fruit trees prune them to keep them down to a height where you can harvest fruit from the ground. This can reduce the water needs of mature trees considerably as the amount of water needed will be related to the volume of the greenery of the tree and therefore the diameter of the tree cubed. Therefore if you reduce the height and width of the green growth of an orange tree by half you will reduce its watering needs by eight provided you have taken steps to improve the soil and mulch to avoid unnecessary water losses.

3. As highlighted in section 4.3 only plant after preparing the soil or compost mixes.

4. If you plan to grow fruit in containers increase the soil fertility and also the growing mediums water holding capacity without it becoming waterlogged. As mentioned in several earlier sections TerraCottem can be very helpful in this respect.

5. When planting ensure that root balls are separated and spread out to ensure that there is a quickly emerging wide network of deep roots to seek out moisture and nutrients rather than a close knit self strangling mesh of spiralling corkscrew roots with a very limited moisture catchment area. This is especially important with citrus trees grown and sold in tall narrow plastic sleeves. When citrus trees self-strangle and become stunted after a few years much water can be wasted by increasing the watering without any effect.

6. Get water down to the lowest roots by a weekly or twice deep soaking versus shallow daily watering. This can be helped by sinking adjacent to the tree a length of five or eight centimetre diameter water tubing or an upturned 1.5 litre water bottle with the bottom cut off and watering into these.

7. Plant through holes in black plastic sheeting. This works well for strawberry plants, red and black currants, grape kiwini and kiwi vines and even fruit trees.

8. Mulch the ground with a layer of compost, peat or coco fibre before laying the plastic sheeting.

9. If you don't use plastic sheeting use a deep mulch around fruit trees that spreads to a metre more than the diameter of the tree. As already discussed in section 4.7 useful mulches include stone chippings, almond or walnut shells, crushed broken bricks from a brick works, composted manures or compost covered with black plastic sheeting.

10. Don't water close to the trunk of a fruit tree. Rather water just outside the drip line of the tree to stimulate roots to spread looking for moisture. Make a moat at this distance from the trunk and water into this to avoid runoff losses away from the tree.

11. If you buy dry rooted fruit trees you should get the whole root system, rather than only part of the root system when roots are cut back by nurseries in order to fit the roots into pots prior to sale.

12. Raspberries multiply by developing new daughter plants on the end of shallow runners. Rather than use plastic sheeting to retain moisture it is preferable to mulch deeply around the canes with compost, comfrey leaves, pine needles, well rotted horse goat or poultry manures or non chemically treated grass cuttings.

13. Ensure that piped irrigation systems water trees according to their type need, age, and years planted. So frequently we come across drought resistant fruit trees, such as figs, still being watered after five or ten years and thirsty plants such as citrus trees in their early years dying because of a shortage of water.

14. You are lucky if you have a grey clay rather than red clay soil as the former retains moisture longer and after an initial watering melons, for instance, are grown without any follow on watering.

15. Often water runs away sideways when watering young fruit tree, especially if the soil slopes. Prevent such water losses by constructing a moat around the tree a little wider than the drip line of the tree and water into this. But make sure that there is an inner mound of earth around the trunk so that the water does not flow against it. If you don't do this trunks can be attacked by fungi.

16. If you wish to plant a lemon tree purchase a perpetual flowering and fruiting variety such as Lunar, Four seasons or Eureka as for most of the year you will not need to water the tree to achieve good crops.

16. If you have a choice buy an early rather than late fruiting variety as you will not need as much summer watering.

17. The earlier books in our Spanish series, Growing Healthy Fruit in Spain and Apartment Gardening Mediterranean Style, will be useful if you decide to grow more than just a token orange tree.

4.13 Growing vegetables

1. Grow miniature varieties of vegetables. They can be planted closer so that roots are shaded, plants are more compact and as each can be eaten fully when first harvested so there is less waste and therefore less wastage of water.

2. Plant plantlets rather than growing all from seed. You won't need to use the water used in raising plantlets to the size required for planting out and you can plant relatively close in blocks to shade the soil and reduce evaporation losses.

3. Grow low growing vegetables around or through taller growing varieties as living mulches to reduce evaporation losses. For instance one can grow melons through /around pepper and aubergine plants.

4. Only grow the amount of vegetables the family can eat, or process/store for out of season use.

5. Don't attempt to grow record breaking sized vegetables. Grow and harvest when younger and at their best.

6. Grow vegetables through holes in plastic sheeting covering rich damp soil. The use of grow bags can achieve the same thing for small numbers of plants.

7. Large plants such as squashes can be grown through holes in old carpets instead of using black plastic.

8. If you have an allotment that is watered by flooding, carpets can be used to cover the ridges between irrigated growing areas and reduce water losses as well as controlling weed growth that uses moisture.

9. Grow vegetables densely in containers such as large size builder's plastic buckets and on growing tables rather than widely spaced in open ground.

10. Except for fruit vegetables grow vegetables in semi or dapple shaded places rather than in full sun. But even tomatoes and peppers do well in dapple/partially shaded situations and ripen over a longer period. The Vi-Aqua technology mentioned in section 4.5 can be of special benefit if growing vegetables in shaded situations.

11. James Lewendon has just reminded me that when he was younger he and his father used to grow amazing crops of potatoes and various types of squashes in large heavy grade black plastic sacks filled with half rotten horse manure with only one small a drainage hole six inches above the ground.

12. Provide shelter from hot and cold winds and hot suns that can cause water evaporation losses by planting live windbreaks of rows of sweet peas, sweet corn, sunflowers and climbing beans. The ears of prickly pear cacti can provide an amazing amount of shelter to emergent melon and squash plants.

13. During the winter and early spring protect frost vulnerable seedlings inside cloches made by cutting off the base of five or seven litre plastic water bottles. A damp nano climate above and below the soil, as discussed in section 4.3, will be maintained and a cane inserted through the narrow top opening and pushed down into the soil will provide stability.

14. Minimise the watering of overwintering vegetables. This not only saves water but produces hardier frost resistant plants. Interestingly after the minus 15 degree centigrade wind factor temperature experienced in March 2005 we lost only a row of peas grown from seeds from Mali. Surrounding commercial growers who watered once or twice a week even in winter lost 95% of their crops.

15. Plant leek plantlets in threes, fours or fives. This way you can grow more leeks per square metre, be able to better weed between growing leeks, harvest easier and moisture is trapped between the intertwined roots of the plants.

16. Don't walk on growing areas as they will consolidate hard and reduce the amount of water absorbed by the soil and increase the extent of runoff away from plants.

17. Use raised beds so that all rain and irrigation water is retained by the friable soil/compost mix that has not been walked on.

18. Grow vegetables in black plastic builder's buckets, growing tables, troughs and other containers.

19. As explained in earlier books 'Growing Healthy Vegetables in Spain' and 'Apartment Gardening Mediterranean Style' the mini growing of a wide variety of vegetables can be very productive in terms of growing areas and water usages.

20. Another way of avoiding the need to walk on soil alongside or between plants is to grow vegetables in strip beds that can be worked from one or both sides. By sloping the surrounding pathways any rainfall will run onto the cultivated soil.

21. Mulch between plants with compost straw or well-rotted manure.

22. If you live in an area where thieving from allotments is becoming common allow grass to grow to partially cover crops such as onions and squashes. This not only hides them and reduces the chance of the theft of crops on which you have used wate,r but also reduces water evaporation and stimulates summer morning dews.

23. MIx a lIttle TerraCottem soil improvemcnt gel into sowing or planting holes or trenches. This can reduce water needs by over 50%. See www.terracottem.com for results of trials.

24. When growing vegetables in containers less expensive alternatives are to mix in cut up sponge, water absorbing types of expanded plastic foam, chopped newspaper or cardboard.

25. If you grow courgettes, melons, pumpkins or other types of squashes the mixing of cut up pieces of segments of prickly pear cacti into the ground ten centimetres below the surface can provide a useful source of moisture and nutrients to young roots. Similarly a buried fish, such as catfish or pike, would be beneficial and provide beneficial nutrients.

26. If you have a spare window box carefully drill two 5 millimetre holes in the bottom and thread short lengths of five millimetre tubing through each hole and glue them in place. Then

thread the base of two tomato plants through the tubes until five centimetres protrude into the window box. Carefully fill up the window box with a rich compost and then plant up the top normally with more tomatoes, peppers or a flowering plant such as petunias which will start to wilt when the tomatoes need watering. Overall it is possible to use less water per kilo of product than normal planting in pots.

27. In summer months grow sprouting seeds, such as cress, mustard, alfalpha, bean sprouts etc., in the kitchen rather than salad leaves in the garden. They require little water especially if you have an automatic watering sprouter.

28. Kitchen water can be used on tougher vegetables such as cabbages and tomatoes provided eco washing up liquids have been used.
29. Swimming pool back wash water can be used, again on tougher plants, provided the pH is below 7.0.

4.14 Growing herbs

1. Make maximum use of the perennial drought resistant narrow leaved aromatic herbs such as garlic, garlic chives, lavenders, lemon verbena, marjoram, rosemary, rue, narrow leaved sages and thymes which like sunny positions.

2. Grow less drought resistant herbs such as mint parsley and stevia in partial shade to reduce watering needs.

3. Grow thirsty annual herbs such as basil parsley and coriander in shady spots to avoid the need for constant watering.

4. Buy small plants that are not already root bound to give one a chance of establishing them without continuous copious watering.

5. Don't over water perennials as they can rot in damp conditions. Just keep the soil damp to the touch until roots are deep when plants like rosemary, thyme and sage will normally not require watering.

6.Grow in free draining non clayey gritty soils to stimulate the development of deep roots.

7. Protect frost vulnerable perennial herbs such as stevia during the winter, as new plants each year require copious watering before crops can be harvested.

8. Use lavender for internal hedges or blocks of plants.

4.15 Growing in containers

More and more plants are being planted in containers on garden terraces, on apartment terraces and balconies and in patios. Not only are flowering plants being grown but also herbs fruit and vegetables.

To reduce the water requirements it is important to recognise that

- Water can evaporate fast through the porous walls of traditional unglazed terracotta containers.
- The root ball of many plants in containers can't go down far so they fill the container sideways and maturing plants become root bound. Soon it is impossible to get water down into the pot and water is lost down the side of the container.
- Water can evaporate fast from the surface of un-mulched soils and composts, especially in full sun.
- If the compost in containers is allowed to dry out it will shrink and a hole will develop between the compost and the wall of the container. When you water it will be lost down this gap until the compost absorbs water and re-expands to fill the gap.
- Commercial composts vary tremendously in quality, especially in their water holding abilities.

Fortunately the following steps can be taken to reduce such losses.

1. Place drip trays under planted up plant pots.

2. Use large pots, window boxes and troughs with built in water reservoirs.

3. Use glazed or plastic containers to avoid evaporation through the sides.

4. If you want to use terracotta containers for their appearance first paint the insides with water impermeable sealant or place a slightly smaller plastic one inside and plant in this.

5. Use containers large enough for at least three years growth so that water absorption is not prevented by a solid root ball, which can cause water to run down the side of, and not into, containers.

6. Use deep containers to allow deep roots to develop.

7. When planting plants in containers leave in the pot you buy but cut out the base before planting up inside a larger pot. This will prompt roots to grow downwards towards a TerraCottem gel improved damp soil layer. This can also be done in the garden.

8. Don't plant anything in other than good quality water retaining, but still well-draining, good compost, peat, palm fibre and soil mixes. It is interesting to fill a number of 30 cm diameter plant pots with different brands of potting composts on a hot day, say 35 degrees centigrade in the shade or above. Place the pot filled with what you consider to be the poorest compost on a weigh scale and note the exact weight. Then pour in water slowly trying to do so evenly across the surface until water runs out of the base of the pot. Then note the wet weight of the pot and compost and calculate the weight of water added.

Then pour in an equal weight of water slowly into to each of the remaining pots in turn.

Place the pots in a line, facing south, and reweigh each pot each two hours until bedtime and again in the morning and continue until each pot has lost the weight of water you had added.

A collation of the results will make interesting reading.

9. Except for pots of drought resistant plants such as geraniums and succulents shade from the hottest suns throughout the year. Low winter suns shining deep into covered terraces can soon dry out containers.

10. Suggestions for the best flowering and evergreen plants for growing in containers in full sun, semi shade, and shade are provided in the book '*Apartment Gardening Mediterranean Style*'.

11. Sink a five centimetre diameter plastic tube down through the compost inside a container to finish a few centimetres above the base of the container and water through this.

12. Mulch the surface of the compost.

4.16 Special ideas for apartment and patio gardens

1. Grow flowering plants, fruit, vegetables and herbs in non porous containers.

2. Thick walled pots keep compost cooler especially when wet after rain, as they take longer to dry out and the process of water evaporation creates a cooling effect.

3. Install shades, blinds and awnings to reduce evaporation water losses.

4. Choose appropriate plants for shade, semi shade and shady positions. Useful plant selections and descriptions are included in my book *Apartment Gardening - Mediterranean Style'*.

 5. Reduce watering needs by growing most vegetables in the shade and during the cooler months. See the watering chart in section 4.8.

6. Install small bore drip feed irrigation to groups of containers. Special mini kits are now becoming available. In our local town there is a champion bonsai grower who has almost a hundred spread over his 300 square metre roof top terrace that has a permanent canvas shade covering the entire terrace. The bonsais are watered several times a day via a micro bore pumped irrigation system and live happily even when the temperature is in the 40's centigrade.

7. Over watering will, in conjunction with over feeding, produce weak plant growth vulnerable to insect and fungi attacks.

8. Groups of containers can shade each other thereby reducing evaporation losses.

9. Don't plant anything except in quality compost mixes. Poor ones rot down and shrink so that the water holding capacity goes and water is lost by fast drainage

10. Mix a little TerraCottem into the bottom half of the compost in all containers. As a reminder your nearest distributor can be obtained via info@terracottem.com .

4.17 Interesting features that don't require any water

The following features can add interest, and in some cases colour. In some instances they will be best set off against a green background of drought resistant evergreens.

1. Colourful mosaic murals or plaques and mosaic covered pots and sculptures.

2. Metal trees decorated with ceramic leaves.

3. Ceramic ornaments of all shapes including balls, eggs, bottles or unusual shaped pots.

4. Bronze, stone, glass fibre or concrete sculptures.

5. Spray painted rock sculptures made from a single or several rocks stuck together. Bronze or gold are good colours.

6. Sun dials on walls or balustrades, or on pedestals.

7. Coloured gates between various areas or mini gardens.

8. A sandy beach corner with a collection of bits of netting, fish net floats, bleached pieces of wood, shells and other beach flotsam.

9. An interestingly shaped dead tree.

10. Childrens corner with sandpit, garden house or tent, swing etc..

11. Areas for quoits, giant chess, petanque, basket-ball, tennis, badminton or table tennis etc.

12. A group of coloured empty pots.

13. An aviary. The birds will drink little water.

14. A chicken run with colourful bantams or national heritage breeds.

4.18 Swimming pools

1. Have no swimming pool or Jacuzzi.

2. Reduce the size of a planned or actual pool.

3. Have a Jacuzzi instead of a pool if your need is just to relax.

4. Buy one of the large Jacuzzis which have a strong current of re-circulating water against which one can swim.

5. As an alternative, reduce the size of swimming pool required to get exercise from swimming by having a small six by two and a half metre pool with a big volume variable pressure recirculation water pump that allows one to swim against the pressure of the current, which can be adjusted to match the ability of the swimmer.

6. Fill the swimming pool and or Jacuzzi with collected and stored rain water. See section 5.1.

7. Cover pools and Jacuzzis when not in use to reduce evaporation.

8. Design pools as emergency water supply tanks for use during periods of severe drought.

9. Install a natural pool, or convert an existing pool. With water purified naturally by passing through beds of natural plants no water is lost by backwashing.

10. Install a tank for collecting back wash water and filter for reentry to the swimming pool or use on the garden.

11. If you are happy to just wade, float and swim but not dive reduce the depth of the pool to a metre.

12. Keep the pool clean during the winter so that it does not need to be emptied, cleaned and refilled each spring.

4.19 Compost heaps

1. If you don't already have a compost heap install one now, for good home-made compost is invaluable in enriching soils and improving their water holding ability.

2. When loading your compost heap in dry climate situations ensure that all materials are dampened layer by layer, with the exception of green kitchen or garden waste which is mostly water any way. This will help produce a compost with a good water holding capacity and attract breeding worms.

3. The above is normally a small problem in temperate climate situations but in dryer Mediterranean climate conditions it is a bigger issue, even during the winter months when day time temperatures can still be in the high twenties and even thirties and it may not rain for months. You can either first dampen material in a builders bucket of water or pour water over each layer as you load the compost bin. This ensures that all layers of material will compost down but not become over wet and slimy. The latter can happen if you remove the cover to the heap during rain.

4. The rain water runoff from the top of our sealed heap is not wasted as we plant, or let self-seed, Swiss chard, tomatoes or squash near the compost heaps. These grow well in the rich moist soil, their roots often growing into the base of the compost heap. This is reminiscent of my grandfather who never used time, compost or water in raising each year's tomato plants. Rather he took me down to the outflow of the village's sewage composter where large patches of strong tomato plants would grow each spring. Interestingly after a spring flood the banks of a local river where I fish were covered in hundreds of tomato plants some of which survived to yield good crops. Small red but firm tomatoes were actually a reasonable bait for carp like using green figs.

5. If it has not rained for some months when you need to turn the composting material do so just before rain or during rain to re dampen the half composted materials. Naturally if the drought continues you will need to physically dampen the half composted material as you turn it, layer by layer.

4.20 Reuse waste water

1. When watering plants in pots place them in a bowl, on a brick in the bowl or on a grid placed over the bowl so that water than runs out of the drainage holes can be reused.

2. Stand potted plants on water collection trays.

3. Collect and use diluted personal night waters, day waters are also possible of course, to water plants in containers. This also fertilizers the plants ecologically, unless you are on strong

chemical medications. As mentioned in Section 4.3 I well remember an elderly lady who had an enviable garden with all the plants in two hundred pots watered this way for years.

4. Use eco car wash liquids and wash the car where used water will flow naturally to hardy shrubs, canes and trees unaffected by eco washing agents.

5. Particularly in rural areas ecological natural toilets that separate liquids from solids can be installed.

6. Recycle house water from washing up, dish washers and washing machines by installing a system comprising a settling tank, irradiation purification unit, aeration pond with reeds and oxygenating plants and a storage tank and pump. Preferably use a solar pump. If you use eco washing agents, and a cool wash cycle, water can be drained directly from washing up machines to the garden.

7. Use eco floor cleaning liquids so that the dirty water in the mop bucket can be used to water the roots of non sensitive shrubs and trees.

8. Cool the water used in vegetable steamers and saucepans to cook vegetables and use the water to water plants in containers, helpfully fertilising them at the same time with leached minerals and vitamins in the cooking water. Cool surplus teas and water from washing fruit and vegetables can also be used.

9. In times of serious drought place the plug in the bath or shower tray before you shower and siphon the water into containers for use in watering plants including geraniums on the bathroom window sill. Likewise if you still take baths. An alternative when taking a shower is to stand in a large washing up bowl to avoid the use of a siphon.

10. Even easier during the warmer months is to set up a portable shower in the garden with a portable plastic mat or wooden slatted square to stand on while showering with cool water.. The portable shower can be moved every day or two to be alongside a number of flower beds or new trees in turn.

4.21 Miscellaneous sources of potential water savings

1. Sweep or use a suction/blower machine rather than wash down paths and terraces.

2. Have a car with a paint colour that does not show the dirt and therefore needs washing less frequently.

3. Design part of the garden as an interesting natural looking dry river bed or pool lined with smooth pebbles and rocks laid over course sand laid on top of unperforated plastic sheeting material which is raised at the edges. In this way, when it rains, you can establish an underground source of water for the roots of an interesting collection of plants, planted to look as natural as possible, along the edges of the imitation dry river bed or pool in buried large pots filled with a gritty compost.

5. 50 IDEAS FOR COLLECTING STORING AND DISTRIBUTING RAINWATER

5.1 Collecting rain water

It is an environmental and economic disaster that much of the 300 to 2000 millimetres of annual rainfall that falls on Mediterranean houses, gardens and allotments is lost and is not of benefit to gardening and growing activities. Since rainfall is free this is a double waste. It's being wasted and one has to purchase water for watering plants. However many things, some simple and expensive, can be done to reduce these worldwide losses.

1. When laying paths around a house or garage leave a space between the building and the path for shrub beds or raised beds that can be watered directly by rain water falling from the eaves.

2. Add gutters and down pipes to as many roofs of the house, garages, greenhouses and sheds as possible and collect rainwater in rain butts or underground and above ground storage tanks located in an under build or large garage, or buried under terraces, paths, drives and swimming pool terraces.

3. If it is not possible to fix guttering due to time cost or availability then in addition to point '1' above place a line of watering cans, empty plastic or metal containers, with the tops cut off where necessary or with funnels placed in their narrow necks, under the edge of the roof to collect as much of the falling water as possible.

4. If plants of any type are being grown temporarily or permanently in containers place them under the roof line to be watered directly by rain water.

5. If you have plants indoors or under a covered terrace place them out in gentle rain to be naturally watered and washed.

6. Locate large plastic or metal water tanks near where rain water could be used and construct a large collection funnel over and beyond the tanks to collect rain water over as wide an area as possible. One sees this in our local mountains with the water used, via a drip feed,. to water new tree plantings or supply water to drinking pools or troughs for wildlife.

7. If you have a number of terraces in the garden or allotment build a permanent or plastic sheeting temporary storage tank below one of the terraces. Cover as large as possible an area of the terrace above with plastic sheeting with the sides and back raised up on soil or rock ridges and the front edge long enough to drop down into the storage tank. Where the plastic sheeting that goes down the terrace wall is wider than the storage tank raise the extra parts up on a similar soil or rock ridge.

8. One could also dig a channel along the base of the lower terrace into which the plastic sheeting from the higher terrace can be hung without the need for a front ridge. The channel can then transport any collected water to the storage tank.

9. When you dig out the hole for a swimming pool double the length and construct covered water tanks at one or both ends of the pool so that rain water can be collected from the terrace around the pool.

We know of one garden with a large pool, large pool terraces that start at the base of wall of the south facing house and large storage tanks under decking covered terraces. There is guttering on the house and the guttering on the south east and west sides of the house lead into the underground storage tanks that all rainwater from the roof is directed into the storage tanks as well as the rain water that falls on the pool terrace. This is an enormous volume even in an area with only 500 to 800mm of rainfall a year. They never run out of irrigation water and indeed purify some water for use in the house.

10. Build a permanent single block wall around your property so that heavy falls of rain cannot runoff into neighbouring properties.

11. Naturally you can't build a wall a cross the entrance to the property but you can ensure that rain water is not lost out of the property or is collected from the outside. For instance if your entrance is at the lowest point of the property slope your drive so that at the entrance it is a little above the height of the outside pavement so that valuable rain water is not lost out onto the pavement or road. Similarly if your entrance is at a low point of the property lower the level of the drive below that of the outside pavement or road and allow outside rainwater to be channelled into your property on a controlled basis.

12. If your property slopes and there is an outside pavement raised slightly or substantially above the level of your soil or paths just inside your property it is possible to install 10 or 15 centimetre plastic metal or terracotta pipes, or just a gap in the outer block wall, to allow some rain water to run from the pavement into your property.

13. If you have a natural gully on your land dam part of it and establish a pond or lake as a storage tank.

14. If it would appear stylish deepen the garden pond and plan to use the extra stored rain water for irrigation.

15. If there is a natural hollow on your land, line it with strong rubber or plastic liner or impermeable clay and collect the rain water that would otherwise soak away or run off your land.

16. Construct channels, or lay perforated drainage pipes, across sloping land to collect and channel excess rain water to where it can be used or stored in collection tanks.

5.2 Avoiding losses of rain water

We have just discussed how to collect rain water but if all the ideas were implemented some could still escape. There is nothing so soul destroying as after waiting months for rain one sees a large proportion of it leave your land or flood uncultivated areas. The following ideas could help in this respect. Most are simple and inexpensive to implement.

1. Take the attitude that 'All the rain that falls on my land is rightfully mine and free'.

2. Install additional above ground or below ground storage capacity so that you don't have to let water over flow when the current water butts and tanks become full.

3. Set up a system that automatically pumps water from almost full tanks to higher up back up tanks so that that water can be run back when necessary for storage, or used to irrigate some of the garden by gravity.

4. If you have terraces raise the front edge of each terrace and slope the top of the soil back towards the base of the terrace above. Rain water will then soak into the soil without running over the front edge.

5. Dig a trench at the base of each terrace wall so that if water should run over the edge of the terrace above it will be held back to soak into the soil. Also in heavy rain excess water could run back into this trench if you slope terraces as in the previous idea.

6. Raise the edges of lawns so that they flood slightly in heavy rainfall.

7. Ensure that the soil in beds alongside paths and terraces is lower than their levels so that rain water runs off naturally into the soil.

8. Place lines of rocks or logs across sloping beds or uncultivated wild areas so that any run off is held back to allow some or all of it to soak into the ground.

9. Slope terraces back from the front edge so that water stays on the terrace and soaks in.

10. Cover slopes with ground cover plants so that runoff is slowed.

11. If you have sloping banks raise the front edge with a stone wall earth bank or rockery to hold running water back.

12. Have a few strategically located wooden boards, fitted with supports to stand them upright, that can be placed across runs of water during heavy rain storms to divert water to where it can be allowed to temporarily flood and soak into the ground. Low cost areas for wet season marsh plants could be created in this way.

13. Mulch as discussed in section 4.7 as many mulching materials are also moisture absorbing.

5.3 Distribution of rain water.

The aim of distributing rain water while it is raining or stored rain water around your land is twofold. Firstly to ensure water only gets to cultivated areas and secondly to ensure that the soil around and beneath the root ball of each plant shrub or tree is always damp to ensure no drying out and continuous growth.

Recognise that for all plants it is the deepest roots that are the most important. These are the ones that stretch down searching out water and nutrients in dry weather, some going metres deep. They are also the ties to hold roots down in windy weather and the ones that survive heavy frosts.

A. Uncollected rainwater.

In most gardens much of the rain fall is not easy to collect and does not end up where it would be of immediate or future benefit. Uncollected rainwater will run everywhere haphazardly unless positive steps are taken. The following practical ideas will help you ensure that this free running water is used to build up the depth of damp earth and eventually the water table under cultivated areas.

We had the first storm of the summer last night but only 15 millimetres of rain fell. Naturally the depth of wet soil in areas only receiving the natural rainfall was very shallow but where extra rainfall had been channeled soil was wet to two to three times the depth.

1. Modify the natural slopes of the land so that runoff water is directed to where it will be of benefit such as flower beds, vegetable plots, orchards or ponds.

2. Slope pathways lengthways and sideways so that while it is raining water is directed to such areas as above.

3. Use solid versus woven plastic sheeting under stone chippings but first modify the slopes and gradients of the land so that rain water can be transported over the black plastic to where best utilised.

4. Pump water from low flooded areas to higher areas. If you have a large piece of land construct an Arab style waterwheel as an interesting feature with buckets to raise water from a low lying water collection channel to a higher one that irrigates growing areas..

5. Dig trenches across slopes of hillside or lawns to direct rain water diagonally to lower growing areas.

6. Construct a cascade of three or four raised beds alongside a sloping or stepped path and divert the water running down the paths onto each level of raised bed.

7. Construct a series of cascading raised beds one above the other so that if one becomes waterlogged the excess water cascades down to the next.

8. If you have a fast draining stony soil that leads to major loses of rain water it is possible to create buried versus raised beds. Dig out trenches eighty centimetres wide by forty centimetres wide to ten metres long or more. Line the excavated trench with strong one metre wide black plastic sheeting and hold down the overlaps on either side with stone or concrete slabs.

Finally before back filling the trenches cut two centimetre diameter circular holes at fifty centimetre intervals for drainage. Pile some stones slates or broken pottery above each hole and then refill the trenches with a compost and Terracottem mix consolidating each thirty centimetres as you progress.

9. Use water dripping off the leaves of an evergreen tree such as a carob tree at the drip line to water a shrub bed that is partially in the semi shade of the tree and partially in full sun.

10. Construct a gently sloping path to within a metre and a half of a newly planted tree with ten to fifteen centimetre sides for the last few metres. From the end of the path bury four 5 or 10 centimetre plastic tubes long enough to take water down to a depth of ten to twenty centimetres below the deepest roots at four points around the tree. Level the top end of the tubes to be level with the surface of the end of the path so that rain water running down the path will fill the plastic watering tubes.

11. Many houses have upstairs terraces with down pipes to drain rain water away. Ensure that this water is directed at soil level to where needed.

B.Distributing stored water.

Naturally the distribution of rain water collected in water barrels/ butts and storage tanks can be controlled. It can be taken to where required in watering cans or run through pipes by gravity or by using pumps.

Water from underground wells and bore holes can be held in tanks or distributed directly by the same means, as can also purchased piped water. Thoughts re piped water distribution are as follows.

1. Where you need to water plants with significant space between each use plastic tubing with adjustable drip water feeds for each plant. Drip feeds result in lower evaporation losses compared to jet feeds.

2. Where there is a continuous line of close plants it is preferable to use continuous woven tubing. Some are rigid while others lie flat when not in use.

3. Use timers at the feed end of irrigation pipes to give you the opportunity of timing watering systems to come on late evening and control the durations and extent of water flows.

4. Aim to water long enough and heavy enough to always keep the lowest part of root balls damp. Once or twice a week watering is generally more effective than shallow watering every day. With shallow watering it is possible for deep rooted plants to dry out and die upwards from the deepest roots in dry weather.

5. Check what is actually happening by digging holes alongside plants, shrubs and trees before and after watering to check the depth of wet and moist soil. Since it can be difficult to assess the dampness or dryness of some soils a dampness meter can be useful. My inexpensive meter measures dampness, pH and light. Meters can be found in good horticultural shops or search the internet.

6. Sink twenty centimetre lengths of five centimetre plastic tubing or upturned 1.5 of 5 litre water bottles with the base cut off alongside large vegetables such as squashes, soft fruit buses, newly planted shrubs and trees and water and liquid feed through these.

7. Proprietary underground large bore pumped and gravity irrigation tube systems can be purchased for watering newly planted tall mature trees.

8. In many cases solar pumps are now preferential to electric pumps for distributing water from storage tanks and butts and for operating water features.

6.0 EMERGENCY ACTIONS

If things become really desperate and there is insufficient water or no water available then desperate emergency needs are required at the household and possibly village/ town or regional/ national level. Here are a few thought starters.

6.1 At the household level

1. Stop using and purifying the swimming pool and use the water to keep the garden going and in really dire straits use for basic domestic use as well.

2. Reread this book and identify ten actions for immediate action. In emergency times this may mean sacrificing the thirstiest plants in the garden, if not already done.

3. Only wash up by hand and do not use the dish washer. Use the washing up bowl of water to flush the toilets or water strong plants.

4. Go back to washing clothes by hand in a bowl and use the dirty and rinse water as above.

5. If still existing use the ancient village washing shed.

5. Use a self standing clothes drier and stand over an area of plants so that the initial dripping of water relieves dry plants.

6. Put up shading over the thirstiest plants including vegetables.

7. Double the volumes of TerraCottem used by digging holes around your special/favourite plants and dropping TerraCottem, or an alternative water absorbing gel, into the holes around the root balls. This can be done likewise with plants in containers or plants can be re-potted with double the normal recommended amount of gel.

8. Steam vegetables and after cooling use the saucepan water to water and feed plants.

9. Collect all night and day waters and use to water and fertilize both container and garden plants. Dilute the personal waters two to ten times if possible with other sources of water.

10. Stop bathing or showering in the bath room but rather set up a portable shower and move it over different groups of plants each time you shower.

6.2 At the village or town level

1. Restrict the days and hours during which the normal water supply is available.

2. Introduce scales of charges which will cost high water users significantly more than economic users.

3. Install stand pipes. It is only a few years ago that this happened in Javea on the Costa Blanca. It led to a desalination plant being installed.

4. Require that swimming pools are only filled with water from rain water holding tanks or purchased lorry loads of water.

5. Require that gardens can only be watered with collected rain water.

6. Turn off all council fountains as a public gesture until they can be operated with collected rainwater.

7. Require that public gardens are only watered with collected rainwater or with water collected in tractor pulled tanks from ancient springs when not being required for agricultural purposes.

8. Remove thirsty plants from municipal gardens and replace by patterns of different colours of stone chippings and rocks and possibly cactii agaves and succulents.

9. Restrict construction activity.

10. Stop washing streets.

6.3 At the regional or national level

Require that all new houses, apartment blocks, council, educational and commercial buildings are built with roof guttering and rain water storage tanks and that this water is used for all tasks other than drinking water.

1. Require that construction systems construct the supporting structure and roof first so that rainwater guttering and storage tanks can be installed early in the construction programme and any water collected be used by the constructors before using the public piped water supply.

2. Require that water rushing down roads is collected through grids and channels and run to storage tanks for later watering of public gardens, washing vehicles, cleaning streets and fire hydrants.

3. Require that historic water collection/distribution systems from ancient springs are maintained or renovated to be used in agriculture, gardens and the uses suggested in point '2' above. This includes the ancient water storage ponds and channel distribution systems.

4. Longer term construct a network of mini reservoirs or large storage tanks to collect rainfalls on mountainsides and in narrow valleys.

5. Establish methods for collecting and storing the enormous volumes of rain water that falls on the runways and plane parking areas of airports.

6. Invest in piped water distribution systems versus open channels.

7. Divert and store the large volume of fresh rain water that swells local and runs out to sea.

8. Authorise interregional water transfer pipes or canals.

9. Organise regional and national competitions with awards to the best ideas and implemented projects. Involve professionals and amateurs, school children through to retired people and all nationalities resident in the country.

7. WATER SAVING GROUPS

7.1 Water circles

Some years ago we wrote a number of articles promoting the setting up of 'Growing Circles' of five to fifteen persons for the growing of day to day seasonal ecological vegetables and fruit. The members to be groups of people living within an urbanization, village, town, street or apartment block, attending schools or members of social groups and gardening clubs etc. The easiest accessible article will be found in the December 2009 archives of our website www.gardeninspain.com.

This concept could be equally applied to the problem of ensuring that more rain water is collected, that the water collecting is put to best private and public use, and that the overall use of water is reduced. Perhaps 'Water Circles' can be promoted productively in various parts of the world.

7.2 Involving the children and elders

How to have a better garden with less water is an issue that affects the whole family so involve the whole family in brainstorming discussions. It is a way of getting children water conscious and with their exploring creative minds they may come up with some novel ideas. Elders will have experienced drought several times in their lives and can perhaps recall what used to be done in the days before piped public water became the norm. Add their ideas to your own and involve both the children and elders in evaluating them all and deciding on the ones which would have most impact, be most affordable and most practical.

7.3 Collecting other ideas

No doubt some readers have additional ideas to those collated from my personal experiences, brain dumping and creativity. If you have any other idea that you would like to make public in half yearly updates of this book please forward it to newwaterideas@gmail.com. Indicating whether you would a personal credit to yourself. Thank you Caroline Harbouri for being the first.

Caroline Harbouri wrote that in the early 1990's she experienced a severe drought in Athens. She ordered anyone, including family visitors, using the shower which was over the bathtub to put the plug in the bath and then after showering immediately siphon the water into buckets using a huge stirrup pump. This provided sufficient water for keeping some precious plants alive. An augur was used to take out cores of soil about 12 inches deep with a diameter of about four inches near to the roots of the plants. The holes were then filled with broken pod shards and/or pebbles and the shower-water and washing-up water from the kitchen was poured directly into the quickly draining holes, so that all the water went straight down to root level. So effective and easy!

More recently in Spain Belgians Yvette La Force and Marie-Claire Delaughe made good progress in starting to turn hard dried out stony abandoned agricultural land into an evolving natural garden by planting several hundred cuttings from friends gardens. When planting the cuttings were 80% buried in the soil and a little TerraCottem was placed at the bottom of each planting hole. Incidentally TerraCottem, which now used widely on five continents in agriculture and horticulture, was originally developed at the Belgium University of Ghent.

8.0 GETTING THINGS GOING AND REVIEWING PROGRESS

Well the scene is set. It is now time to start to analyse and act on your own situation. There are many things to consider and act on so do start now rather than wait until you are in the middle of the next period of dry weather or even officially declared drought. But don't attempt to do everything overnight. Do take prioritising as discussed in Part 2 seriously so that sensible and continuous progress can be made. Review progress from time to time to evaluate the benefits to date and the next priorities to tackle. Best of luck with your endeavours

For those that like formal action plans we attach a convenient format as appendix 2.

9.0. DON'T GIVE UP IF RAINS COME!

In April 2012 1 visited the garden and allotment of my daughter Sophie in Hove England. Like we in Spain she had had no rain for months and a hose pipe ban had been announced that day to commence immediately. I spent an hour on the allotment discussing with her and other allotment holders what could be done to immediately keep existing plants going, prepare for spring sowings and survive the summer as the ban suggested that restrictions would continue for many months until reservoirs were restocked.

Since I had just written an article on the topic of waterless gardening for a number of papers and magazines in Spain I promised to send her a copy to put on the notice board of the allotment shop once I arrived back home in Spain. En route I visited dry gardens in Belgium but it started to rain, then gardens of Mediterranean Gardening Society Members in the south of France where they were as desperate for rain as we were in Spain. Phone calls to friends in Andalucia and Cataluña in the south and north of Spain, plus the island of Mallorca, and further afield to Italy and Greece indicated that all the Mediterranean Coastal plains and inland mountains and valleys were suffering. Other calls and emails to family and friends in Mediterranean climate zones of Australia, South Africa and USA confirmed that similar problems had been experienced in recent years.

The next day I started to write the first draft of this book as there seemed to be a general need that would continue forever, even though some years we would have droughts and others plentiful rain. Indeed by then my daughter had phoned to say that the allotment was flooded and the hose ban lifted and since then England has experienced record levels of rain for two years. The article was never sent off as she would have a complimentary copy of this book and friends could eventually obtain copies via Amazon Kindle.

As I finalise the text for this book here in Spain, and in other situations around the Mediterranean Sea, this year's drought has not yet broken and many readers will find an immediate use for the book in planning for next year.

The book is intended to be timeless. Something to be taken out of the bookcase when it is next raining to initiate actions in advance of the next drought or to look for ideas for immediate implementation should you already be again in drought.

The long term shortage of water is unlikely to ever go away even though rain, the foundation of growing things, is free.

Happy waterwise gardening worldwide to all readers.

Dick Handscombe

La Drova, Spain

May 2014

Appendix 1

Collecting and prioritising ideas

Key : H=High agreement with statement, M= Medium agreement, L=Low agreement

Number of idea	Page in book	Brief description of idea	Potential for reducing water use H,M ,L	Ease of taking action H, M, L	Low cost of taking action H, M, L	Overall priority for action H, M, L
1.						
2.						
3.						
4.						
5.						
6.						
7.						
8.						
9.						
10.						
11.						
12.						
Etc.						

Appendix 2

Action plan to improve gardening practices

Action no.	Page in book	Brief description of action to be taken	Likely benef-its H,M,L	Cost esti-mate L,M,H	Plan to		By whom	Done
					Start	Finish		
1.								
2.								
3.								
4.								
5.								
6.								
7.								
8.								
9.								
10.								
11.								
12.								
Etc.								

Appendix 3

A useful starter list of the more drought resistant plants

This list is based on the plants described in our earlier books 'Your Garden in Spain' and 'Apartment Gardening – Mediterranean Style', plus a few plants introduced into our garden later. The botanical and common English names are given.

A list of the wild plants that existed on our terraced plot when we moved into the just completed house is also provided as Appendix 4. Many still exist alongside the plants brought in by purchase, growing from seeds, propagated from cuttings, dropped by birds or blown in from surrounding gardens and woods.

A.Annuals – Spring annuals are shallow rooted and won't survive without moisture in the soil in gardens or in the wild. Soil needs for most – Very fertile, rich in humus, water retaining but well-draining. Success can be enhanced by mixing a water retaining gel into base of planting holes. This can reduce frequency of watering from two or three times a day in full sun in July and August to every two or three days.

In our area of Spain the nearest to a drought resistant plant is the wild poppies that still spring up after months of drought. Others spring up after a storm. All annuals purchased or grown from seed require frequent watering.

B.Perrenials – Many perennial put down deep roots and once established can be considered as highly drought resistant. We would include the following as the most drought resistant as they will be found in deserted gardens or are successfully left by absentee gardeners without leaving an irrigation system on.

General soil needs – fertile, rich in humus, water retaining and free draining.

Acanthus mollis, Acanthus

Coreopsis, Calliopsis

Osteospermum fruticosum, African daisy

Euryops chrysanthemoides, Paris daisy

Gaura lindhemeri, Gaura

Heliopsis, Orange sunflower

Iberis sempervirens, Everlasting candytuft

Leonotis leonorus, Lion's ear

Leucanthem vulgare, Oxe eye daisy

Malva alcea, Holyhock

Pelargoniums, peltatum, regal, graveolens

Strelitzia, Bird of paradise

Salvia leucantha, Velvet sage

Salvia splendens - Red flowered bush

Salvia Perovskia, Russian sage

Salvia pratensis, Wild meadow sage

C.Culinary and aromatic herbs - Annuals all need regular watering, as will many perrenials. The herbs that will survive with long periods of drought are those that are found in the wild. General soil needs are fertile, gritty, free draining and non- clayey.

Alcèa rosea – Hollyhock

Alliums, Chives and garlic chive

Armoracia rusticana - Horseradish

Aloysia triphylla, Lemon verbena

Artemesia absinthium and ludoviciana, Wormwood

Borago officinalis – Borage

Chamaecyparissus - Santolina

Hypericum perforatum – St John's wort

Laurus nobilis, Bay

Lavandulas - Lavenders: Angustifolia officinalis; Intermedia, English; Dentata, French

Melissa officinalis – Lemon balm

Origanum vulgare- Golden oregano

Origanum majorana – Sweet marjoram

Rosmarinus officinalis, Rosemary

Rumex acetosa – Common sorrel

Ruta graveolens, Rue

Salvia officinalis, Common sage

Salvia argentea, Silver sage

Santolina, Cotton Lavender

Thymus, Thyme – Various varieties

Valeriana officinalis, Cat's valerian

D.Ground cover plants – We have tried many ground cover plants as part of our living mulching philosophy but all need moisture several times a year. Some we use, like Alpine strawberries to warn us that a dapple shaded area is starting to dry out.

General soil needs are enriched soil, moisture retentive and well-draining.

The most drought resistant are as follows.

Carpobrotus, Giant pig face

Helianthemum caput felis – Yellow rockrose

Crassula multicava, Fairy crassula

Dicliptera suberecta –Justice

Erigeron karvinskianus- Fleabane

Fragaria vesca – Wild strawberries

Iberis amara and sempervirens– Everlasting candytuft

Lantana montevidensis, Trailing lantana

Juniperus horizontalis – Spreading juniper

Sedum rubrotinctum – Christmas cheer

Tradescantia . Tradescantia

Vinca major, Greater periwinkle

E.Flowering shrubs – Most shrubs are moderately water resistant so they need watching. They will be most drought resistant if weaned off frequent watering so that their roots are encouraged to go deep rather than remain stunted or grow sideways. General soil needs are as for perennials except for acid loving plants such as rock roses and hydrangeas.

The most drought resistant from our experience are as follows.

Atriplex halimus – Saltbush

Buddleja - Buddlieja

Callistemons - Bottlebrushes

Cistus - Rock roses of various types

Grevillea - Grevilleas various

Helianthemums – Various rock roses

Hibiscus rosa sinensis and syriacus - Hibiscus

Lantana camara - Lantana

Myrtus communis - Myrtle

Nerium oleander- Oleander

Plumbago auriculata – Plumbago, Leadwort

Polygala dalmaisiana, myrtifolia - , Sweet pea shrub

Ricinus communis – Castor oil plant

Rosa, Rose – with deep roots

Spartium junceum – Spanish broom

Teucrium fruticans – Bush germander

Viburnum tinus phyladelphus – Mock orange

F.Climbing shrubs – There are many climbers seen in Mediterranean gardens but those originating from subtropical and temperate sources are only moderately drought resistant even when well established. General soil needs are as perennials. We have found the following to be the most drought resistant.

Bignonias: Campsis grandiflora, Chinese trumpet creeper ; Pandorea jasminoides, Bower vine ; Podranea ricasoliana, ; Tecomaria capensis, Cape honeysuckle

Bougainvillea glabra – Blougainville- purple and scarlet

Blougainvillea Buttania – Buttania – large flowered reds, oranges etc..

Crispum jasminoides – Solanum, potato vine

Fallopia, Russian or mile a minute plant

Hedera, Ivy

Lonicera, Honeysuckle

Jasmins officinale, Common; Polyanthum, polyanthum; Nudiflorum, winter

Passiflora caerulea – Passion flower

Pyrostegia venusta - Brazilian flame vine

Rosa, Rose – with deep roots

Solandra - Chalice vine

Solanum - Potato vine

Vitis vinífera - Grape vine

Wisteria - Wisteria – in our valley there is a hundred metres of hillside covered with a wild plant which smothers a long ago abandoned orchard.

G. Bulbous plants

Soil needs are generally high in humus and free draining. It's best to place a thin layer of grit under bulbs when planting. The list below is based on what has flowered well during the recent dry year with no watering but flowering season would have been longer with spring rain or watering.

Agapanthus, Lily of the Nile

Amaryllis, Belladonna lily

Bletilla striata – Chinese ground orchid

Crocus, crocus – including Crocus sativus - azafran

Croccossmia Lucifer - Crocossmia

Cyclamen – wild cyclamen in shade of trees

Eremurus robustus- Foxtail lily

Freesia - Freesia

Gladiolus illyricus - Wild gladioli

Hemerocallis - Day lily

Iris - Irises: Germanica, Common flag; Xiphium, Spanish; Xyphium tingitana, Dutch

Ixia nerines, Ixias

Liliums - Lilies: Asiatic, Asiatic; Candidum, Madonna; Lancifolium, Tiger; Regal, Regal;

Mirabilis jalapa - Flower of the night

Muscari - Grape Hyacynth

Narcissus - Daffodils large and miniature

Ornithogalum narbonense - Ornithogalum

Polygonatum biflorum – Solomans seal

Scilla peruviana - Peruvian scilla.

Tulbaghia violacea - Society garlic

H. Succulents

Soil needs to be gritty or sandy, rich in humus and free draining. Succulents benefit from a mulch of fine stone chippings or ground volcanic ash to keep stems dry.

Aeonium – Aeonium

Carpobrotus – Giant pig face

Carpobrotus edulis – Cat's claw

Cheiridopsis – Lobster claws

Cotyledon – Cotyledon

Crassula – Crassula

Dudleya farinose – Live for ever bluff lettuce

Echeveria – Echeveria

Euphorbia peplus– Milk weed spurge

Euphorbia myrsinites – Donkey tail

Gibbaeum – Gibbaeum

Graptopetalum – Graptopetalum

Huernia schneideriana – Dragon flower

Jovibarba – Jovibarba

Kalanchoa tomentosa, pinnate etc., - Kalanchoes

Kniphofias – Red hot póker

Mammillaria – Pin cushion cacti

Mesembryanthemums; Aptenia - Aptenia, Delosperma – Messem, , Drosanthemum Candens – Rosea ice plant, Lampranthus – Ice plant

Sedum spectabile- Ice plant

Sempervivum – Sempervivum

Senecio articulatus – Candle sticks

N.B Although all are, in our experience, drought resistance many are not frost resistant. Therefore those kept in a potted collection around a sunny terrace are placed inside a temporary green house from November to March . Also cuttings are taken and potted up in the autumn of most others in case garden planted varieties are lost to heavy frosts.

I.Cacti, Agaves, Aloes and Yuccas

Soil needs as succulents.

Astrophytum myriostigma - Bishop's cap

Carnegiera gigantea - Giant saguaro

Cereus - Cereus

Chamaecereus - Peanut cactus

Echinocactus grusonii - Golden barrel cactus

Echinocereus - Hedgehog cactus

Echinopsis - Sea urchin cactus

Epicacactu - Orchid cactus

Epiphyllum oxypetulum - Orchid cactus

Ferocactus - Barrel cactus

Gymnocalycium - Chin cactus

Haageocereus - Haageocereus

Mammillaria - Pincushion cactus

Opuntia ficus indica - Prickly pear

Opuntia microdasys - Bunny ears

Opuntia subulata, Pole cactus

Parodia - Ball cactus

Rebutia - Crown cactus

Agave Americana - Century plant

Agave attenuata - Agave attenuate

Aloe vera - Aloe vera

Aloe arboresens - Red hot poker

Aloe melanacantha - Aloe melanacantha

Aloe saponaria - Soap aloe

Yucca aloifolia – Spanish bayonet

Yucca elephantipes – Spineless yucca

J.Grasses and bamboos

Cortaderia selloana, Pampas grass

Dasylirion, Bear grass

Festuca glauca - , Festcue

Miscanthus. Ornamental grass

Pennisetum, Fountain grass

Phyllostachys aurea, Fishpole bamboo

Cyperus involucratus, Umbrella sedge (Not a bamboo but like one)

K.Hedges

Berberis, Barberry

Bougainvillea glabra, Bougainvillea glabra

Callistemon, Bottle brush

Cupressus leyandii, Leyland cypress

Euphorbia millii, Crown of thorns

Lantana camara, Lantana

Laurus nobilis, Bay or Laurel

Lavanda, Lavander

Ligustrum, Privet

Myoporum laetum, Good-for-nothing

Oleander nerum, Oleander

Pittosporum tobira, Japanese mock orange

Rosmarinus officinalis, Rosemary

Teucrium fruticans, Bush germander

Viburnum, Viburnum

L.Flowering trees – There are many wonderful flowering trees and many are very drought resistant once established. Many others are moderately drought resistant and survive well with watering in hot weather. Those trees we regard as drought resistant are as follows. General soil needs are as perennials.

Acacias, Wattle

Arbutus, Strawberry tree

Bauhinia, Orchid tree

Cercis siliquastrum, Judas tree

Crataegus monogyna - Hawthorn

Euphorbia pulcherrima, Mexican flame tree

Ginkgo biloba, Maiden hair

Jacaranda, Jacaranda

Justicia adhatoda, Justice

Melia azedarach, Bead tree

Nerium, Oleander

Nicotiana glauca, Cigarette tree

Parkinsonia aculeata, Jerusalem thorn

Platanus orientalis, Plane

Prunus dulcis, Almond

Robinia pseudoacacia, False acacia

Schinus molle, False pepper

Schinus terebinthifolius – Brazilian pepper tree

Tamarix tetrandra, Tamarix tetrandra

Tilia platyphyllos, Tiila

M. Fruit and nut trees and bushes – General soil needs are deep and fertile, rich in humus, moisture retaining but free draining.

Easiest to grow in dry conditions are as follows.

Armeniaca vulgaris, Apricot

Carissa macrocarpa, Natal plum

Carya peca, Pecan nut

Carylus avellana, Hazelnut

Ceratonia siliqua, Carob

Citrus limon, Lemon

Citrus Sinensis, Orange

Citrus reticulata, Mandarin

Citrus paradisi, Grapefruit

Citrus tangerina, Tangerine

Cydonia oblonga, Quince

Diospyros kaki, Persimmon

Eriobotryra japonica, Loquat

….

Punica granatum, Pomegranate

Ficus carica, Fig

Persea gratissima, Avocado

Pinus pinea, Pine kernal

Pistacia vera, Pistachio nut

Prunus amygdalus, Almond

Prunus sativa, Plum

Juglans regia, Walnut

Malus silvestris, Crab apple

Morus nigra, Mulberry

Olea europaea, Olive

Opuntia ficus indica, Prickly pear cactus

Passiflora edulis, Passion fruits

Phoenix dactylifera, Date palm

Prunus spinosa, Sloe

Ribes nigrum – Black currant

Rubus fruticosus, Blackberry

Tilia platyphyllos, Tila

Viitis vinifera, Grape vine

N.Evergreen trees – Generally as perennials but some prefer a more acid soil.

This list is related to dry south facing situations where other trees are moderate in respect of moisture needs. More can be grown on north-west facing slopes in northern hemisphere and deep in shady valleys.

Abies, Fir tree

Acacia, Wattle - various from seeds and cuttings, some lost with frosts

Araucaria, Norfolk island pine

Ceratonia, Carob

Cupressocyparis leyandii, Leyland cipres

Duranta erecta – Golden dewdrop

Eucalyptus gunnii, Cider gum

Magnoliagrandiflora, Magnolia

Juniperus, Juniper

Pinus halepensis, Aleppo pine

Pinus nigra martima, Corsican pine

Pinus pinea, Pine nut pine

Pistacio vera,Pistacio,

Quercus ilex, Holm oak

Taxus, Yew

O.Palms, Yuccas and Cordylines

This how we grouped them in the book 'Your garden in Spain

Soil needs are rich in nutrients, high in humus, sandy and free draining.

The easiest ones to coach deep roots and little to no watering are as follows.

Palms

Chamaerops humilis, Mediterranean fan palm

Cycas revoluta – Sago palm

Phoenix canariensis, Canary island date palm

Phoenix dactylifera, Date palm

Phoenix reclinata, Senegal date palm

Phoenix roebelinii, Dwarf date palm

Livistona chinensis, Chinese fan palm

Washingtonia filifera, Cotton palm

Washingtonia robusta, Mexican fan palm

Yuccas, Cordylines

Yucca aloifolia, Spanish dagger

Yucca elephantipes, Spineless giant yucca

Yucca gloriosa, Spanish dagger

Cordylines australis, New Zealand cabbage tree

Appendix 4

Indigenous plants growing on and around original wild abandoned agricultural terraces which became our garden.

In the early holiday making only years they were the mainstay of the garden and would have continued to be if I had not been asked to write gardening columns and then books. At this stage the range of plantings was expanded considerably in order to write from first-hand experience for all types of expatriates and all types and sizes of gardens.

Many still exist amongst today's mixed collection of plants.

Trees

Almond- Prunus amygdalus

Carob – Ceratonia siliqua

Fig – Ficus carica

Olive – Olea europoea

Pear – Pyrus communis

Pine – Pinus pinea

Shrubs

Black thorn, sloe – Prunus spinosa

Oleander – Oleander nerium

Pistacio – Pistacia lentiscus

Ground cover

Aptenia – Aptenia

Cat's claw - Carpobrotus

Rock roses – Cistus albidus, parviflorus, monspeliensic

Stone crop - Sedum acre

Bulbs

Wild garlic - Allium nigrum

Asphodel – Asphodelus fistulosus

Grape hyacinth - Muscari

Wild gladioli - Gladiolus illyricus

Iris flag – Iris germanica

San Diego - Mirabilis jalapa

Narcissi – Narcissus tazetta

Orchid – Orchis italica

Urginea maritima, Sea squill

Succulents/Cactii

Agave - Agave americana

Aloe- Aloe arboresens

Aptenia - Aptenia

Optuntia indica – Prickly pear

Optuntia microdasys – Bunny ears

Optuntia subulata – Pole cactus

Stone crop – Sedum acre

Yucca- Yucca optunia

Annuals/Biennials

Holihock – Alcea rosea

Poppy – Papaver rhoeas, dubium

Sweet pea –Lathyrus clymenum

Climbers

Blackberry – rubus fruticosus

Fragrant clematis – Clematis flammulla

Honeysuckle – Lonicera etrusca, implexa

Ivy – Hedera helix

Herbs

Agrimon - Agrimonia eupatoria

Asparagus – Asparagus officinalis

Bay – Laurus – nobilis

Borage – Borago officinalis

Chicory – Cichorium intybus

Dandelion – Taraxacum officinale

Fennel – Foeniculum vulgare

Hound's tongue – Cynoglossum officinale

Hyssop - Hyssopus officinalis

Mint – Mentha spicata

Rosemary – Salvia rosmarinus

Rue – Ruta graveolens

Sage – Salvia officinali

St John's wort – Hypericum perforatum

Thymes – Thymus serpyllum, pipirella, pebrella

Valerian, red – Centranthus ruber

Verbascum – verbasum chaixi

Wild rocket – Eruca vesicaria

Appendix 5

List of some other gardening books by Dick Handscombe

*Jointly with his wife Clodagh

All are most conveniently obtained from Amazon books and other internet bookshops.

Your garden in Spain - From planning to planting and maintenance*

Apartment Gardening – Mediterranean style*

Growing healthy fruit in Spain*

Growing healthy vegetables in Spain*

Living well from our garden – Mediterranean style

Authentic Valencian Paellas – Using mainly garden produce

CPSIA information can be obtained at www.ICGtesting.com
Printed in the USA
LVOW09s1751170416

484034LV00017B/323/P